ASHT

SPT

MAKING WORK FUN:

Doing Business With a Sense of Humor

by Ron Garland
Foreword by Karl Albrecht

Shamrock Press
910 Grand Ave,
San Diego, CA 92109
(619) 272-3880

This book was composed by Joe Coyle in 12 point Adobe Palatino Prepress and book design by Joe Coyle

Cartoon Credits

© 1977 Henry R. Martin; used by permission

H. Martin; reprinted by permission: Tribune Media Services

© 1986 by Sidney Harris—"What's So Funny About Business?"

William Kaufmann, Inc., Los Altos, Calif.

Ashleigh Brilliant epigrams, Pot-Shots and Brilliant Thoughts; used by permission of the author, Ashleigh Brilliant, 117 West Valerio St., Santa Barbara, Calif. 92101

William Hamilton; used by permission of the author

Robert Mankoff; reprinted by permission of UFS, Inc.

Library of Congress Cataloging in Publication Data

Garland, Ron
Making work fun: doing business with a sense of humor.

1. Managers 2. Humor 3. Organizational behavior
FOREWORD
ISBN 0-913351-10-5

Dedication

To Henry Martin, whose delightful "Good News/Bad News" cartoons help me start each day. Every morning, before I read the sports, before I check the stocks and bonds, and before I read the news of the world, I turn to the Business Section of the San Francisco *Chronicle* and start my day with a good chuckle.

Foreword

It seems to me that the ultimate purpose of any business enterprise ought to be to enrich the lives of human beings — its owners, its customers, and its employees. Profit (at least in the commercial sector), goes without saying, but any profitable business that fails to contribute net value to human life is a failure, no matter what the balance sheet says.

A sense of humor goes a long way in all aspects of life, and work is no exception. We all need to laugh, and especially we need to be able to laugh at ourselves. Psychological research and common-sense experience both tell us that the first tell-tale sign of overstress is losing your sense of humor. And getting it back again proves you've gotten your stress under control.

Well, here comes Ron Garland, a guy who has devoted years to making his own work and the work of other people fun. This is not a book about why to have fun — it's a book about how to have fun, fun, and more fun. He begins — and I agree completely with him — with the premise that the right of all human beings to have fun, yes, even on the job, is inalienable and inarguable. It even pays off for the business, but that's entirely secondary.

What you'll see here for your enjoyment is one guy's own unique, individual view of fun. He shares with you over 101 specific things you and the people you work with can do to make working there fun. You won't like all of them; you'll probably even dislike some of them. But that's the wonderful thing about fun; it's so individual, and yet it can be shared.

If you're a bit prudish or stiff-necked, or if you're one of those self-appointed defenders of all ethnic and demographicß groups against "stereotypical humor," you'll probably find a few things here to get indignant about. And that'll be some fun for you.

As the publisher of this book, I feel quite comfortable in having it be one guy's world-view on fun, with his own particular biases, quirks, — and, yes, even stereotypes. Because that's the way humor is. The best joke is one that pokes fun at the human condition, but not at the condition of any one human. It's done in good spirit.

I hope you'll have some fun just reading this book. I'll bet it will begin to have a subtle effect on your thinking. You surely won't try all of the ideas here, but if you use even a few of them, I think you'll have your money's worth and then some.

So sit back, relax, get into a fun mood, and see what one of America's best "funologists" has to share with you.

Have fun.

Karl Albrecht

Contents

x

INDEX OF FUN IDEAS

Acknowledgements

Special thanks to all my friends who read early drafts of this book. They gave me the benefit of their input and even helped me select cartoons out of the thousands in my files.

Thanks to J.G., L.D., D.D., and S.M. for encouragement. Thanks to Steve Albrecht for all his hard work on the final edit. Thanks to all the people from around the country who read my first management book and wrote to encourage me to do a "sequel."

Thanks to all the fools I have worked with over the past twenty years; their craziness forced me to develop a good sense of humor to survive.

And thanks to Rhonda for making me laugh every day, no matter how many managers and union officials have called me an idiot or worse.

What People Are Saying About Work

"There is a new ideal about work emerging in America today. For the first time, there is a widespread expectation that work should be fulfilling — and that work should be fun...For millions of baby boomers, this new ideal is not outrageous; it is natural. Affluent and extremely well-educated, they grew up believing life should be fun — and work, too."

John Naisbitt and Patricia Aburdene, *Reinventing the Corporation*

"Work that is neither fun nor meaningful is not worth doing well, no matter how much one is paid to do it."

Russell L. Ackoff, *Management in Small Doses*

"One of play's products is fun — one of the most powerful motivators around. I've noticed that a fun working environment is much more productive than a routine environment. People who enjoy their work will come up with more ideas. The fun is contagious, and everybody works harder to get a piece of that fun."

Roger von Oech, *A Whack On the Side of the Head*

Society's New "Central Project"

"The required new thinking, compatible with emergent values emphases, can be simply stated: In a technologically advanced society where production of sufficient goods and services can be handled with ease, employment exists primarily for self-development, and is only secondarily concerned with the production of goods and services. This concept of work represents a profound shift in our perceptions with implications that reverberate throughout the entire structure of industrial society."

Willis Harman, *Global Mind Change*

Warning!

If you haven't engaged in any strenuous fun at work within the past twelve months, please don't implement any of the ideas in this book prior to consulting with your physician. The laughter and joy may be too intense for your weary heart.

INTRODUCTION

In my book *Working and Managing in the New Age*, I listed the fundamental elements of what I called "New Age Management." Of the elements listed, the one that has received the most reaction is "fun." Several people have asked, "How can we create more fun in the work place?"

In the seminars and workshops that I present, "fun" is also a favorite subject. Due to the high interest in this topic, I decided to devote an entire book to the subject of fun in the work environment. This is not a sequel to my earlier book noted above, but the concepts are related.

This book is an elaboration on one aspect of the New Age Management techniques. You need not have read the earlier book prior to reading this one, but the two are related and I would certainly recommend you read the other book at some point.

There are two reasons for my recommendation: First, I would appreciate the royalties. Second, while fun is important, it can't replace the other aspects of New Age Management. If you have a repressive work environment, these fun ideas will be of little value in and of themselves. You must first lay the foundation by adopting a whole range of progressive, holistic approaches to management. You can't pay your employees peanuts, treat them like dirt, and then expect them to be happy just because you're willing to let them have a little fun now and then.

On the other hand, if you treat your employees like human beings, give them respect, show consideration for their needs, help them develop and find meaning in their work, then these fun ideas will be a valuable part of your total effort to create a positive work environment.

In sum, a little fun won't make up for a lot of abuse, but a little fun can be a valuable ingredient to a managerial approach that treats employees with dignity and respect.

"Emily, I've just cleared my desk and am taking the afternoon off."

CHAPTER ONE

FUN: Why, Who, What, Where, How and How Much

Question #1: Why should work be fun?

Answer #1: If you have to ask, you'll never understand.

Question #2: Who needs fun?

Answer #2: Everyone.

Question #3: What is fun?

Answer #3: Please refer to the answer to Question #1.

Question #4: Where should we have fun?

Answer #4: Here, there and everywhere.

Question #5: How do we have fun at work?

Answer #5: A good question. Please refer to chapter 4.

Question #6: How do we know when we've had too much fun?

Answer #6: When you die laughing.

Question #7: Are there any scientific studies that prove a fun work environment is really more effective?

Answer #7: I'm sure there are, but I don't want to know about them. I'm interested in having fun. If you can't have fun until you find a study that shows it's okay, then you're in deep - - - - .

This book is for people who believe that life should be fun and that work should be fun. I won't spend much time or effort to convince you of this philosophical premise. If you're old enough to read this book, you undoubtedly already have your own philosophy of life, and if you didn't basically agree with my premise, then you probably wouldn't be reading this particular book anyway. So I won't waste your time telling you what you already know.

There are several philosophical approaches you can take toward life (and work). You may feel that life is meant for fun, or that life is meant for suffering, or that life is a test, or some variation or combination of these ideas. I won't try to sell you on one philosophy over another. I will, however, share with you, very briefly, my own philosophical bias so you can understand the premise for the specific ideas that follow.

I believe that life should be fun. I believe that work should be fun. I believe that life presents a wonderful opportunity and should be enjoyed and appreciated. I am very grateful to the Divine Force for allowing me this opportunity. I plan to show my appreciation by making the most of it. I believe that a fun work environment is more conducive to efficiency and creativity and likely to reduce unnecessary stresses.

Fun is like art. It's hard to define, but I know it when I see it. The dictionary defines fun as "something that provides mirth or amusement; enjoyment, playfulness." A secondary definition notes that fun is "playful, not serious."

I believe this secondary definition is the cause of a great deal of misunderstanding about fun. This book is titled *Making Work Fun*.

Yet I did hesitate to use that title since the word "fun" means so many different things to different people.

I teach a workshop called "Making Work Fun" and have noted many differing definitions of fun. Several people, especially serious corporate executives, have recommended that I not even use the word at all. One businessman stated, "When I first saw your workshop advertised as 'Making Work Fun' I had no intention of attending it. I thought it would be frivolous and irrelevant to the real world. However, several people I respect recommended the workshop very highly and stated it was the best one they had ever attended. So reluctantly I agreed to go, and they were right. It's great and it's relevant. And in retrospect, I can see that the title is perfect for the class, but I think most people will misunderstand it — just as I did."

The gentleman was right. While the title of the workshop is perfect, most people misunderstand it because they assume, per the secondary definition from the dictionary, that fun is not serious. Fun is very serious. Fun is what life is all about. Without fun, why bother? Fun is good for the soul. Fun is good for the work environment. Fun is good, period. We should not feel ashamed of having fun. It is not a waste of time to have fun. Fun provides the spark that keeps the flame of life burning bright.

However, if the word "fun" continues to present a problem for you, change it to something else with which you're more comfortable or just drop it. Instead of "fun ideas," think of the following ideas as ways to increase morale, reduce stress and boredom, stimulate creativity, and create a positive work environment.

The primary definition of fun lists "playfulness" and "enjoyment." Life should have these aspects, and so should work. We should approach life playfully and we should approach work playfully. We should get enjoyment from life and from our work. If you agree, read on. If not, stop here because what follows will prove very annoying to you.

CHAPTER TWO

What Should Be An Employer's Primary Objective?

Ask an employer this question and you will likely get an answer along the lines of the following, "To make money." Ask managers at most companies, they will likely say, "To make money" or "To increase profits and productivity." Ask a union leader and you will likely hear, "To provide job security for all employees." Ask an employee and you will likely hear, "To pay me a decent wage."

However, I, with my twisted hedonist world view, would argue that all the above answers (important though they may be) are really the means towards an end and not an end — certainly not the primary objective. I maintain that the primary objective of most employers should be to provide the members of the organization(including managers and employees at all levels) a high quality work environment.

A high quality of work life would by necessity include good pay, job security, profits, high productivity, etc. However, it would also include much more. It would include fun, meaning, and an opportunity for personal development.

Let me repeat this point just in case you can't believe what I said. The primary purpose of an organization should not be profits or efficiency. The primary objective of an employer should be to create a better life for all members of the organization. Profits and efficiency are important, even essential. But they are a by-product, a means, or a secondary objective, not the primary objective.

This idea may seem startling to some people, but expand the concept to life itself and not just to work and see if you don't agree. Is the primary purpose of life to make money? Or is the primary purpose of life to find meaning and happiness? A reasonable amount of money is necessary for happiness, but money is a means, not an end. I believe the same is true at work.

I believe if employers understood this concept and applied it we would revolutionize the work environment. If an organization really put people first — put people ahead of profits — it would be a great place for everyone to work. There would, of course, be profits, but not an obsession with profits.

In making any decision, the first question should be "Will this improve the lives of the members of our organization?" A gain in efficiency or profits that comes at the expense of lowering the quality of people's lives is seldom a worthwhile gain. It's important to understand that people enjoy being efficient and making money provided these goals don't become obsessions that are carried to extremes. So it is reasonable to expect people to work hard, have high productivity and help the company earn a profit. It's not reasonable to expect that they will do this if it isn't producing a positive, rewarding life style for them.

The ideas that follow will help make work fun and create a positive work situation where people understand that profits and efficiency are important, but the real reason to work is to have the kind of rewarding, enjoyable life they want for themselves.

When we puts profits and efficiency first, it's easy to lose sight of people and the result is an all round disaster — no profits, no efficiency and a poor working environment. When we put people first, profits and efficiency will still receive their due and the result is an all around success — good profits, high efficiency and an enjoyable working environment. So why not have some fun and have it all?

THREE IMPORTANT WARNINGS:

1. Don't try to do everything. There are over a hundred fun ideas listed in the following pages. If you implemented all of them at the same time, your group would turn into a three ring circus. Some of the ideas will be appropriate to your people; some will not. Be selective and choose those ideas most likely to receive a favorable reaction from your specific group of employees.

2. First, do the basics. Remember what I said in the "Introduction"? You did read my nice little "Introduction" didn't you? If not, that's okay. Many people skip introductory sections. Here's the main point repeated: Fun cannot replace basic human decency. You must first practice progressive management techniques that involve treating your employees with respect and dignity. If you treat your employees like expendable units of production and pay them a substandard wage, these fun ideas will not help morale. However, if you treat your employees like human beings, pay them a fair wage, and follow progressive personnel policies and practices, then these fun ideas will be a major factor in creating a positive, fun work environment that will increase productivity, increase creativity, and reduce stress.

3. Some of my suggestions may be illegal. Don't assume that I know anything about the law whatsoever. Even in the area of my expertise, labor law, I am occasionally wrong. Outside of this area of the law, you should assume that I know nothing. In the waning

days of our neo-Puritan society, there are still many laws designed primarily to restrict you from having a good time and still many sourheads whose twisted idea of fun is enforcing these laws and preventing others from having fun.

As I stated, I believe work should be fun. I also believe that reading books about making work fun should be fun as well. Therefore, I've tried to make this book fun by including some of my favorite work related cartoons and by my writing style. I hope you'll agree that this is a fun book to read, but don't let the cartoons, the jokes and my semi-serious tone mislead you. This is a serious book. I hope you'll give these ideas serious consideration and implement several of them in your organization.

CHAPTER THREE

101 Specific Ideas for Creating Fun in the Work Environment

There are literally thousands and thousands of ways to make work more fun. Some are general and apply to almost any organization, and some are quite specific and would only be useful in a particular type of organization. The ideas I am including in this section tend to be of the general type that could be used by many different types of businesses, companies, corporations, factories, and public organizations.

These are largely ideas that I have personally used, personally developed, created during my workshops on fun in the work environment, or in some cases, simply stolen from someone else; theft being the sincerest form of admiration. Please feel free to steal these ideas from me and use them. You can even pretend they were your own.

Fun Idea Number 1

Put Cartoons on Your Interoffice Memos

I have used this approach for years with wonderful results. The mechanics are easy. Have your memo prepared as usual. Have it signed, dated, etc. Then, before you have it photocopied for distribution, select an appropriate cartoon. If possible, the cartoon should be related to the subject matter of the memo, but any humorous cartoon will do.

I keep a cartoon file with thousands of cartoons indexed by subject matter. Whenever I see an especially good cartoon in a newspaper or magazine, I cut it out and add it to the cartoon file. You can also buy books with collections of cartoons or check them out of the library. Make photocopies of your favorites and add them to your file. Depending upon your business and the subject matters you deal with, you may need different types of headings. Some of the subject matter headings I use are — Bad Management, Unions, Negotiations, Corruption, Stupid Work Practices, Holiday Themes, Sex, Meetings, Business Travel, Expense Accounts, Family Situations, Tardiness, Politics, etc.

Once you've selected an appropriate cartoon, make a photocopy of your master copy. Find a place on the memo (the front page or last page is usually the best) where there is some blank space to add the cartoon. If the cartoon is too large for the space, use the reduction feature on your photocopy machine to reduce it so it will fit. You may need to reduce it two or more times (in effect, reducing your reductions), but don't make it so small that people can't read it.

Then, cut out the copy of the cartoon you will be using and do your paste up using a glue stick. Just smear a little on the back of the copy of your cartoon and stick it on the memo in the proper space. Now you can photocopy and distribute the memo.

There are several advantages to this "cartoon-on-the-memo" approach. First of all, most people will enjoy the cartoon and it may make their day a little more pleasant and increase their morale just a tad. Secondly, it will certainly increase the likelihood that they will read your memo — which is why you're writing to them in the first place.

In addition, the cartoons can sometimes be used as hard evidence. For example, when I was manager of an Employee Relations section, I added cartoons to all my staff memos. One day, I approached one of my employees to inquire about a certain legal point. Frankly, I was about to admonish the employee for preparing an inadequate response to a legal motion. The employee alleged that he was unaware of the recent court ruling which had changed this part of the law. I just happened to notice a cartoon he had placed on the wall of his office (the same cartoon I had placed on my memo to the staff explaining this particular court case). When I asked him where he got that cartoon, he immediately acknowledged that it was from one of my memos.

Moments later, realizing he was now trapped, he admitted that he had seen the memo after all. Of course, this can work both ways. Beware! Don't get caught with a cartoon on your wall from a memo you don't want to acknowledge having received.

You can see I love cartoons. I'm taking the same approach with this book that I take with my memos. However, there are a few words of caution you need to keep in mind (beyond the possible copyright infringements from stealing and reproducing cartoons). Never use a cartoon that could be offensive. Stay away from anything involving racial or ethnic stereotypes. Don't use anything with sexually explicit language or drawings. I enjoy reading

Playboy, but I steal most of my cartoons from the *New Yorker*. Also, avoid anything politically specific. It's okay to use a cartoon making fun of politicians in general, but not one attacking a specific candidate (unless of course, your organization is in politics and the cartoon attacks one of your opponents). Finally, avoid anything that might offend people based upon their religious ideas.

Fun Idea Number 2

Amusing Anecdotes Required for Speakers and Trainers Giving Presentations

This is an idea that I stole from a labor relations conference in Los Angeles a few years ago. One theme of the conference was that good labor relations begins with good entertainment. They had a rule along the lines of the following: "Any individual desiring to speak at this conference must precede his or her remarks with an amusing anecdote or some other type of entertainment directly or indirectly related to the subject matter on which they seek to speak."

The theory behind this was simple. People in the labor relations business (including labor relations officials, human resource officials, arbitrators, mediators, union officials, etc.) sometimes tend to become very pompous, adversarial, and verbose. Since this was a joint union-management conference — the major theme was improving labor-management cooperation — and there were hundreds of pro-union and hundreds of anti-union people present, the potential for conflict and verbal sparring was extremely high.

There was a significant possibility that the whole conference could degenerate into three days of stupid, self-serving speeches. It was almost certain that any speaker at the podium would be subjected to many negative remarks and sarcastic questions during the question and answer period following the speech. It was also felt that most of these questions would not be sincere efforts to seek information or clarification, but would really be a not so thinly disguised attack on the speaker's position.

Therefore, the "required anecdote" guideline was adopted for the conference. It accomplished several valuable objectives. By requiring the speakers to begin with humor (many told truly humorous jokes) or a form of entertainment (some speakers did magic, some juggled, some sang) it defused a lot of hostility. The speakers, even those presenting unpopular opinions, became more human and were less likely to be personally ridiculed.

The whole mood of the conference was festive and up and played perfectly into the theme of cooperation. Each new speaker was eagerly greeted as the audience was anxious to see and hear what they were going to do.

Stuffy speakers and people with no sense of humor decided not to speak to the conference and saved everyone a boring speech. (A sub-theory was that anyone who couldn't tell an amusing story or do something entertaining was probably so devoid of creativity that their speech would be worthless anyway.) So the speeches at the conference were generally excellent.

Since people in the audience also had to tell a joke or do something entertaining before they could ask a question, most of the brainless twits who normally dominate a Q-and-A period remained quiet and the questions that were asked tended to be interesting and relevant and not just self-serving attacks on the current speaker's position.

It was far and away the best conference I have ever attended. Subsequently I (and many other groups) began to use a similar approach at our meetings, conferences, and training sessions. It has been so successful that I think most organizations should use this approach for virtually all conferences and training sessions and many meetings as well.

I have seen a number of variations on this theme over the past three to four years. Some groups have a rule that permit someone to ask a very brief question (30 seconds or less) without having to do something special to get the floor — provided the question is routine (such as, "Would you please repeat your last statement? I didn't catch point number four."). This seems like a reasonable exception and you may want to make other exceptions depending upon your group and your specific type of gathering. Of course, people will need advance notice.

At quick, informal meetings, this process would be inappropriate. In addition, you may want to make exceptions for special guest speakers on occasion. However, the overall concept is very valuable and I urge you to try it, especially at preplanned conferences, training sessions, and meetings with formal presentations.

You may think that you would have trouble telling stories or doing something entertaining, but it's much easier than you might expect. Let me give you a few examples of things I have done.

Anecdotes are the easiest. You can get books at the library or at bookstores that list thousands of stories and jokes. You can write your own. You can use real life stories. You can steal a joke from one conference and tell it at a different one. Material is everywhere. Just open your eyes and ears. Remember the funny stories you hear from your friends.

You can videotape Johnny Carson's monologue every night and steal his jokes. You can subscribe to a comedy newsletter which will send you new jokes every two weeks. If you don't know how to tell a good story even after you have one, there are books and classes to teach you how to improve your technique.

Here are a few of my favorites. Keep in mind that I spent several years in labor relations representing management and while I have encountered numerous people in unions who are intelligent and honest and decent, I have also had many conflicts with irresponsible unionists who wouldn't know the truth if it bit them in the butt. These people have caused me to develop a high degree of cynicism about union officials. Therefore, some of my personal material tends to make fun of unions (although I have tons of material which makes fun of management as well).

Some people will consider this a sexist joke, or one in bad taste. That's a matter of choice; many people don't. I won't apologize for my sense of humor, but I respect your right to your own. Just skip it if you get angry about these types of jokes. I like it.

This story involves one of my favorite cities, San Francisco. Unions have always been very powerful in the city. San Francisco has also always been something of an "open" city. There have been many legendary "tenderloin" streets, houses and madams in San Francisco's history. Sally Sanford, the Barbary Coast and other names immediately spring to mind. Even today in San Francisco there are areas where almost every other house is what is called a "House of Negotiated Pleasure."

It has been said that many labor relations types frequent these houses in order to practice their skills — of negotiation of course. Anyway, it is in such a district that this story takes place.

A man went into a House of Negotiated Pleasure and asked the Madam, "Is this house unionized?" She responded, "No sir. It is not." He said, "Well, then I will have to take my business elsewhere because I'm a union man. I've always been a union man. I will always be a union man and I only support unionized businesses." And he left and went up the street to the next house.

At the second house, he asked the Madam the same question and got the same negative answer. He again responded, "Well, then I will have to take my business elsewhere because I'm a union man. I've always been a union man. I will always be a union man and I only support unionized businesses." And he left and went up the street to the next house.

Well, the Madam at the second house was very quick-witted. She telephoned the next house up the street and advised them that a "union man" was on his way. When the man reached the third house, he again asked the Madam, "Is this house unionized?" And the Madam replied, "Yes sir, it is." The man said "Great! Because I'm a union man and I only support unionized businesses. I can do my business right here."

So he took a look at the "girls" that were all lined up for inspection and he saw a young blonde that he found especially attractive. He said to the Madam, "I'll take that young blond."

And the Madam replied, "Sorry sir, but you'll have to use the old redhead because she has 30 years seniority."

This story got excellent reactions at several training sessions and conferences and even union officials have told me they love it. I used it to preface remarks about the folly of using seniority for work assignments and promotions as well as to introduce more general discussions about the negative aspects of any number of union proposals and demands.

The following is another story I use to introduce my training sessions on negotiating techniques. Just to make sure there's a sense of balance, this one makes the man the butt of the joke.

This wealthy couple had suffered some setbacks in the stock market. They needed to adjust their household budget. They sat down one night after dinner to negotiate some adjustments in their spending patterns. During these discussions the husband said to his wife, "You know, if you would just learn to cook, we could fire our cook and save $20,000 a year."

And the wife replied, "Yes, that's true. And if you would learn to make love, we could fire the chauffeur and save an additional $30,000 a year."

I then point out two important negotiating tips using this story. From the husband's side, you must be careful what proposals you put on the table for they may generate a counter-proposal that you would rather not deal with. In negotiating, as in playing checkers or chess, you must look a few moves ahead. From the wife's side, you must be careful how you structure your proposals or you may disclose information to the other party via your proposal which would have been better kept confidential.

I could go on and on with these stories. I have hundreds of them, but I think two should be enough to give you the idea of how you can use an amusing anecdote to lead into and help make your points.

Many people don't like to tell stories and prefer to do other entertaining things to preface their remarks. Here are several alternatives you might want to consider:

Let's start with magic. I frequently do magic in my presentations to make my point. I had to train over a hundred managers on a new union contract. I had not negotiated the contract myself, but I had to do the training. The contract was very bad for management. The union had won major concessions. The managers already knew enough about the contract to know it was a sell-out and they hated it. They knew I didn't negotiate it, but I was there in the auditorium and I was going to be training them.

I would be an easy target for their criticism — most of which I would agree with, but agreeing or disagreeing at this point was irrelevant. Our job was to learn the contract, not condemn it.

I started my presentation by doing a trick. I took a balloon and gave it to a manager. I asked her to examine it to make sure it was just a regular balloon. Then I asked her to blow it up, tie it, and return it to me. She did this and then I said, "I know many of you think the new contract is a sell-out, but this is untrue. The idea that the new contract is a disaster is a myth."

At this point, of course, I was getting a few boos and hisses from the audience who thought I must be an idiot if I didn't understand that the new contract was in fact a disaster, especially for these first-line supervisors. I then said, "I'm going to prove to you that this idea that the new contract is a disaster is a myth and I'm going to do it symbolically. Let's say that this balloon represents the myth that the contract is bad for management. And let's say that this three-foot needle represents the facts."

At this point, I pulled out a very long and very sharp needle. I then said, "I am going to take the facts represented by this needle and burst the myth represented by this balloon." I then carefully inserted the needle into the tip of the balloon, and the balloon didn't burst.

The audience usually reacts at this point with some sense of disbelief. I then thrusted the needle all the way through the balloon and out the other side (where the balloon is tied). At this point, I held the balloon with a long needle going in one side, all the way through and out the other side.

The audience usually reacts strongly at this time in amazement. I said, "Well, I can see that this particular myth is going to be very difficult for me to burst today before this particular audience." I then pulled the needle all the way through the balloon and out the other side so that I held the needle in one hand and the balloon in the other. Seeing the needle pass through and out the balloon with the balloon still intact sent another minor shock through the audience.

I then said, "Well, maybe it's not a myth after all. What if we turn the myth back into a balloon and our questionable facts back into a regular needle and see if we can burst the balloon that way." Now I stuck the needle into the side of the balloon and it immediately burst.

After this, the audience is on my side. They know that I know that the contract stinks and they have enjoyed the trick, which is rather amazing the first time you see it. I have done it dozens of times and I'm still amazed that it works myself.

The trick is a great introduction for the training. What's most amazing is that it's a very easy trick to do. It's just a question of putting the needle through the two pressure points on the balloon. You can do it using any balloon (except helium filled ones) and any long, sharp needle lubricated with oil. For best results, get the special balloons and needles they sell at magic stores.

The key to your magic is the magic store. There are dozens of very impressive tricks which anyone can learn to do in five minutes or less. The secret to good magic is to have the right equipment and use some imagination.

So go buy a few magic tricks at your magic store. Practice them on your spouse and kids and find a way to use them to introduce your presentations.

Other ideas for introductions include juggling, singing, dancing, etc. I used to play a lot of basketball and can do some fancy dribbling. For one presentation, I came out on stage and put on a dribbling exhibition, bouncing the ball through my legs and behind my back a few times. The audience wasn't expecting it and it definitely got their attention and applause. Once I brought my badminton racket and hit a few birdies into the audience. Afterwards, I stated that this was probably the first time many of these managers had ever actually seen any service from anyone in the labor relations department.

Here's one final example: If you can't think of anything else, play a tape for the audience — either audio or video. I've introduced presentations about the Olympics by playing a tape of the song, "Chariots of Fire." I've introduced presentations on very trivial matters (which I somehow got stuck talking about) by playing a video tape of the Mickey Mouse Club song. You remember, M-I-C-K-E-Y M-O-U-S-E, Mickey Mouse™. I've introduced presentations around Christmas by showing the music video of "Grandma Got Run Over by a Reindeer." Of course, I came out to introduce the video wearing a reindeer costume.

There are literally "zillions" of ways to inject humor and entertainment into your speeches, training sessions, conferences and presentations. I urge you to try something new for your own presentations and consider making it mandatory for everyone at some of your organizations's formal conferences, meetings, and training sessions. Not only does humor and entertainment make the gathering more enjoyable, but people are much more likely to remember your point if it's made with humor or in some interesting manner.

The importance of humor in presentations has long been recognized. Many top executives have staff writers who write jokes and stories for them. Other novel ways of making presentations interesting and enjoyable are becoming more and more common as well. According to the *Wall Street Journal,* Bill Herz, President of Magicorp in New York City, earns up to $1,000 an hour to teach executives one or two simple magic tricks to do during their business presentations. Mr. Herz charges up to $50,000 to coordinate an entire production with major illusions. For example, he taught an A & W executive how to make a can of root beer "float" for use at a sales meeting in Scottsdale.

Fun Idea Number 3

Work to Music

I love music. I think music is one of the most wonderful things in the universe. I agree with Nietzsche who said "Without music, life would be a mistake." I wake up to a musical alarm clock. I brush my teeth to music, shave to music, shower to music (a special waterproof radio), eat to music, drive to music, jog to music, make love to music, read to music, write my books to music, and go to sleep to music.

Yet, I frequently work in repressive, deprived environments where music isn't permitted. This silence forces me to sing a lot and I'm not exactly Sinatra.

I'm convinced that I work better with music than without it. I think the same is true of many people, certainly those of us born after 1946 who were raised on rock 'n' roll and who studied with music in the background. There are no sure fire snap analyses you can do to determine whether a particular work environment is good or bad, but the presence or absence of music is as good a single measure as I've ever found.

Show me a work environment that permits employees to listen to music while they work and I'll show you a work environment that is probably positive in many other aspects as well. Show me a slave pit where the company will not allow the employees to listen to music while they work and I'll show you a business that is almost certainly negative on every other important aspect.

I understand that some jobs are incompatible with music, and that in some cases music could be a dangerous distraction causing potential safety hazards. But most jobs, especially in offices, are fully compatible with music. There are essentially three approaches a company can take: One is to ban music completely. Another is to provide background music — usually called "elevator music." Some people find this worse than nothing. I don't like it either but personally think it's better than listening to the air conditioning system. Another option is to allow employees to play their own type of music.

This is certainly the preferred approach. It can be done where employees have private offices or cubicles. In offices with "open space" design — that is, where there are no walls — then obviously you can't have everyone playing their own music. The solution here may be to allow employees to listen to whatever they want so long as they use headphones or Sony Walkman-type radios and tape players so their music doesn't bother others.

If headphones are not practical — where employees must spend much of the day on the telephone or talking to each other — it may be possible to cluster groups together who like the same type of music, like jazz or classical and have them share one sound system.

One issue that inevitably comes up is whether employees should be restricted to music or allowed to listen to anything they want, including ball games, "soaps," talk shows, Senate hearings, etc. This is not an easy question to answer. Studies done for advertising agencies have shown that music is a "background" sound that doesn't generally interfere with attention.

However, "talk programs" of any type including ball games, call-in and news shows, soaps, etc., are "foreground" programs and do tend to retain people's attention and could therefore interfere with work. I doubt you would want to broadcast a talk show over your office wide sound system (unless you wanted people to stop working and listen).

On the other hand, if people are using headphones, they will

Fun Idea Number 4

Install Televisions in the Break Areas

Why stop with radios and tape players? Let's really get into the Modern Age. If we are talking mass communications, if we are talking electronics, we are talking T and V. Now, even I admit that it's difficult to work and watch TV. Television isn't a good background device. It tends to absorb your attention. Frankly, I don't especially like TV, but many people do. I even know a couple of reasonably intelligent people who like to watch daytime soaps. So although it hurts me to recommend this, a lot of employees would appreciate and enjoy having access to a TV at the work site.

Many companies have installed TVs in the break rooms and lunch rooms and allow employees to watch the tube during non-working periods. This can be a good morale booster and help make the work environment a little more enjoyable for those who like this sort of thing. My put downs of people watching TV are not meant to be malicious. Sad to say, I watch far too many hours of TV each week myself and the fact that most of it is news and sports does not make me feel any better about it than if I were wasting my time with Vanna White.

Fun Idea Number 5

Play Telephone Tag

Telephone tag is a game for organizations that want to keep employees at their desks and also increase communications among them. It works like this. Let's say that I am "it." I call Joe. Joe is at his desk. Therefore, I can't make Joe "it." I also can't admit to Joe that I'm "it." So I have to talk to Joe about something. Joe and I discuss the production schedule for next month. We hang up. I call Mary. Mary is away from her desk. It isn't break time or lunch time and Mary is not in an officially scheduled meeting. I leave Mary a message. "You're it."

When Mary returns from the snack bar or restroom or wherever, she learns she is "it." She must now call people in the office and try to catch someone away from their office. If they answer, she must find some issue to discuss with them and not acknowledge that the purpose of the call is just to "tag" them.

In practice, many people will recognize that you are probably "it" and playing "tag," but you can never admit it even if it's true — else you lose. The game continues until the end of the day. The person who is last "it" or anyone who violates a rule during the day must bring in doughnuts or coffee or something for everyone the next morning and start the next day as the first person who is "it."

This sounds a little stupid, I admit. And in some organizations, it would be counterproductive in the extreme. However, other organizations have used it successfully. It can be played continuously day after day, or played one day a week or one day a month. The goal is to get people talking to each other and encourage people to stay in their offices near their phones. If these objectives aren't necessary for your office, then the game would not be appropriate. But many organizations do want their employees, at least in certain departments, to stay in their offices as much as possible and communicate with other employees around the organization as much as possible to share information and discuss what is going on. If these objectives fit your job or department, then "telephone tag" may be a good option for you.

You can have all kinds of rules and variations. You can play for a weekly bonus. You should not be able to "catch" someone when they would normally be away from their desks — such as during scheduled breaks and lunch and other times when you know in advance that someone will be away. But you can change the rules to fit your situation and accomplish your specific objectives.

"Good morning, vice-presidents!"

Fun Idea Number 6

Play Computer Tag

This game is very similar to telephone tag except it's played in organizations where the office has an interfaced computer system linking numerous employees. In our computer system, this is called a "LAN" or Local Area Network. All this really means is that I can sit at my desk, push a few buttons on my terminal, and send messages to one more of my co-workers. I can send these messages anywhere in my office or across the nation to one of our other offices using E-Mail (electronic mail).

It offers a way to encourage people to stay at their terminals. If you get caught away from your terminal, you are "it" and you must send out queries and try to catch someone else away from their screen.

Again, the game can be played daily, weekly, monthly or whatever. There can be prizes or bonuses or penalties. The variations and options are numerous and should be adapted to fit your organization's specific needs.

Fun Idea Number 7

Put Cartoons On All Handouts at Training Sessions and Presentations

This idea is similar to Fun Idea Number 1 where we discussed putting cartoons on interoffice memos. Once you have established your cartoon file, you may discover many work-related uses for it. I have been putting cartoons on all my training handouts for over a decade. This can be done for formal training sessions, presentations at conferences, briefings, informal presentations to your staff, etc.

Almost anytime you have a piece of paper you need to pass out to a group of people you should consider adding a cartoon related to the subject of the handout. The overwhelming majority of people will enjoy the cartoon and it makes your handout more valuable and more likely to be retained.

For example, I have found that when I distribute a piece of paper at some type of presentation without a cartoon on it approximately one-third of the audience will not even take the paper with them. They'll leave it lying on the table or on their chair. When I add a cartoon to the same piece of paper, 99.9 percent of the people in the audience will take the document.

Whether they ever look at the document again or not, I can't say, but I'm relatively sure they will look at it at least one more time — when they cut the cartoon out and add it to their own cartoon collection.

Fun Idea Number 8

The Weekly Quiz

Most people love to play games. Most people like to show off how much they know. Most people also like to win things. You can use these facts to help make your work environment more fun. Once when I managed a small staff of eleven, I had a weekly quiz, game or contest. The winner of the contest got a prize. It was usually a book (that I wanted them to read anyway), a record, a tape, a balloon, a box of candy, a bottle of wine, etc. The prize changed every week. It was always something of real value, but nothing too expensive.

The weekly quiz, game or contest was also different each week. This allowed everyone a chance to win. If one week's quiz was on something you knew nothing about, next week we would be playing something different. The staff looked forward to seeing what kind of game I would devise each week and what the prize would be.

During a presidential election year, I would have them predict the winners and percentages of the candidates in the various primaries. The person who came closest to the actual finish was the winner. During the World Series, I would have them predict the winner and scores. During the Olympics, I would pick out several events and use those. In April of each year, I would have them predict who would win the major academy awards. Of course, I also used the Super Bowl, basketball playoffs (college and pros), football bowl games, Grammys, Emmys, etc.

Some weeks if nothing of particular interest was happening in the world, I would just create a quiz. I'd select five or ten questions on some topic. The quizzes were usually questions I had taken from a magazine or newspaper, although I would hold the article for several weeks before I used it, just in case anyone had seen it. One week we had a "Mickey Mouse" quiz consisting of a series of questions about Mickey. I discovered the questions and answers when I took my four year old daughter to Disneyland. I have used many famous people for quizzes as well, including Elvis, John Lennon, Bob Dylan, Prince, Joan Baez, and Madonna.

If worse came to worst and I totally ran out of ideas (or more likely ran out of time) for a particular week, I could fall back on how many jelly beans are in the candy jar or have a "little lottery." A little lottery is where each staffer picks numbers for the weekly lottery and gave the numbers to me (but no money). The person who got closest to the winning numbers won my little prize.

Again, the possibilities are endless. This was an inexpensive way to have some fun. It took very little time, cost only a few dollars a week, and gave the staff something to look forward to.

This is also something that is effective on a one-time basis as part of a presentation or training session. I frequently start my briefings or training sessions with a quiz — usually just one question. The first person to get the right answer wins a small prize of some type. I try to select a question or prize related to my topic.

For example, when I teach a seminar on "New Age Management," I may ask, "Who wrote *The Aquarian Conspiracy?*" or "Who wrote *In Search of Excellence?*" The winner gets a free copy of my book *Working and Managing In the New Age.*

Depending upon the size of the group and the length of my presentation, I may have three or four such quizzes scattered throughout the day. If you think about it, I'm sure you can find many work situations where a quiz or contest would be fun.

Fun Idea Number 9

Office Luncheons

Let me be honest. I don't like office luncheons. But this is not a list of things that I enjoy. This is a list of specific ideas that you might want to consider for your organization. And many people love office luncheons. Therefore, despite my personal reservations about this idea, it is something that many offices use effectively.

Now there are several ways to approach this. One way is for your group to all go out together to a restaurant. This is my favorite, which is to say the least objectionable. But this is not what most people think of as an office luncheon. Most people think of eating together in the office itself.

There are at least three ways to approach this method: One is the pot-luck. Everyone brings something from home (maybe meat, veggies, dessert, bread, whatever) and shares with the group. The other option is to get take out food. Order some pizzas, Chinese food, tacos, whatever. Lastly, you can have a group birthday party for everyone. Some larger offices celebrate a group birthday party once per month, where you can give small gifts or cards to the people having a birthday during that particular month.

However you do it, the event is fairly similar. You all sit around together, eat and make polite conversation. It's a world of fun as many of you probably know. Seriously, despite my personal cynicism, many people do like these things, and thus I have participated in many of them. They do provide a good opportunity for the staff to talk to each other, laugh with each other, dump food on each other, trade recipes or discuss movies and restaurants, and develop a more friendly, relaxed atmosphere.

So just because you have been to a few of these in one office and you hated them and everyone else hated them doesn't mean that these luncheons wouldn't be effective morale and team builders in a different office with a different group. At least consider the idea. Just, please, don't invite me.

Fun Idea Number 10

Group Games

This is another idea many organizations use. This is generally an optional after-work activity, but depending upon the particular game, it may be possible to play at work during lunch or breaks. The types of games run the full gamut of games themselves. You can organize bridge teams, chess clubs, basketball teams, softball teams, volleyball teams, video game competitions, tennis teams, table tennis matches, golf teams, etc.

There is an underlying theory which explains why organizations use many of these activities. The theory is that these activities build team spirit or company spirit, increase morale, develop group loyalty and cohesion, make people more human to each other (especially activities involving managers and employees both), and thus make working together smoother and more effective. These activities are also fun in and of themselves and it's generally good for employees and managers to have fun together. The good will that is built during these activities can help overcome some of the tension from the inevitable conflicts and disagreements in the office itself.

Accordingly, I recommend this approach for most organizations. However, you must be alert and aware. This approach can backfire. If you have highly competitive people who compete against each other in the office (perhaps to meet sales quotas or production quotas) and they carry this same high level of competitiveness over into the basketball games or mixed tennis tournaments, these outside activities may have the effect of making employees hate each other even more. To many people "games" are not games. They are very, very serious matters and they would rather cheat, lie, steal or kill than lose. If several people in a group have this approach, the activities may turn into "war games" and the office into a war zone. Be careful.

Some organizations like to take people who compete against each other in the office and put them on the same team for the games and perhaps play against other companies. This may work. However, people have an amazing range of reactions to the same events. If people don't get along at work, playing together on a team may bring them closer together or may cause them to blame each other for the team's failure. Or it may cause them to compete against each other for the glory of leading their team to victory. It's seldom simple.

Many of these group games are appropriate for co-ed participation. Softball is a good example. However, where men and women are playing games together on the same teams, management (or the team organizers) must be sensitive to the different levels of skill and varying degrees of competitiveness. Although there are many exceptions of each sex, you will likely find that as a rule, men are much more competitive, even to the point of being considered "ruthless jerks" by the women. Usually the women are more likely to play "just for the fun," which is, in these situations, the real purpose.

I have seen success in many mixed softball leagues where each team has an equal number of men and women. This balances out the skill level and makes the games less intense and more fun.

These games should make the work environment more pleasant, more friendly, and more relaxed. If they aren't doing this (or if the games are doing just the opposite), then cancel them.

Fun Idea Number 11

Theme Days

There are dozens of possibilities here alone. Let me just give you a few examples of what I'm talking about. Let's begin with food. How about Chocolate Day? Or Garlic Day? Or an office Ice Cream Social? Each person on the staff brings his or her favorite ice cream and shares it with everyone else. For the ice cream social or chocolate decadence day, it's best to do this at break time. For something like "Garlic Day," everyone brings a dish they especially like with garlic and it becomes a pot-luck luncheon. (Here's a quick quiz for you: Do I like pot-luck luncheons? Yes or no? Very good, just wanted to be sure you were paying attention.)

Since my great weakness is desserts, I especially enjoy theme days built around ice cream, chocolate, pastries, etc. But theme days don't necessarily have to center around food and eating. You can focus upon clothes. You can have a 50's day and everyone dresses accordingly. How about an office "toga party" or a Blue Day where everyone wears something blue? Or a "color" week, blue on Blue Monday, green on Friday (payday), with appropriate colors for the other days as well. Or a "Western" day. Use your imagination. The possibilities are almost unlimited.

Fun Idea Number 12

Costume Contests

This idea is similar to the theme day above, but offers additional variations. You can have costume contests where the winner gets a small prize. You can have a "theme" such as the 50s, 60s, Christmas, Halloween, even a formal "Black Tie" contest. Or the contest can be open with all types of costumes permitted on the same day.

One office I worked in had an annual Halloween costume contest where literally hundreds of people would dress up in a wide variety of costumes. Over lunch, everyone would go to the auditorium and the contestants would parade across the stage. There were official judges and formal prizes. It was a fun day and almost everyone looked forward to it, even the many employees who didn't come in costume.

Speaking of those who do not participate, it's important for most of these "fun ideas" that participation be optional. There may be situations that require total participation, but these situations should be minimized. To the extent possible, all these activities should be truly optional so that those who don't wish to participate don't have to and don't feel bad about it. The purpose of these ideas is to make the work environment more pleasant and not to make people feel bad.

Fun Idea Number 13

Movie Charts

I love movies. Most people do. Movies are a great escape. Until I became a parent, I used to go see virtually every movie that was released. Now things are different. I don't have time to go to the movies three nights a week. In addition, getting a baby sitter is always a hassle. So now I must be much more selective in choosing which movies to see. If I get to two movies a month, I'm lucky. I don't want to waste my time on a second rate movie. I don't even have time for the 6s and 7s. I want the 8s, 9s and those rare 10s (like *E.T., The Big Chill,* and *Gandhi*).

But how do you know in advance if a movie is really any good? Reviewers are one way. And if you're talking professional movie critics, then you're talking Siskel and Ebert. Siskel and Ebert have revolutionized the movie review business. Before Siskel and Ebert, I used to read the movie reviews in the magazines and newspapers. Half the time, I couldn't tell what the movie was about or if the critic even liked it. The critic was so determined to impress me with his or her knowledge of movies that he or she didn't bother with the basics — what's it about and whether it's recommended.

Siskel and Ebert with their simple yes/no, thumbs up/thumbs down style have changed this. Now even most of the air-head movie critics spend a little time explaining what the movie is about and throw in at least a line or two indicating a favorable or negative rating. In fact, Siskel and Ebert have spawned more clones than most hit movies. Everyone is copying their format. But they are still in a class by themselves.

Still, I don't always agree with them. And sometimes they disagree with each other. When Siskel says it's one of the year's ten best, and Ebert says the screenplay needed substantial revisions, what can you do? What I do is ask my friends who see lots of movies. I find my co-workers are excellent movie critics. I had a friend named Bill who was an excellent movie critic. Although he liked horror movies and I don't, on almost every other type of movie, his recommendation was almost always on target. I would frequently check with him to see if he had seen a movie before I went to see it. After he got promoted and left our organization, there was a serious void in terms of reliable movie recommendations.

It was at this point that I thought of the idea of a movie chart. It works like this: You make a list of all the major movies from the past several months in one column and a list of all the employees on your staff (or those who see movies) in the other column. You have lots of empty lines to add the new movies as they are released. Whenever anyone on the staff goes to see a movie, they then fill in their space on the chart with a rating from 1 to 10.

By comparing your ratings with those of your co-workers, you will quickly get a good idea of which people on your staff share your taste in films. These people can then be your guide and you can be their guide in selecting which movies to see.

This movie chart is very inexpensive. It just requires a few pieces of paper and a small amount of space to post the chart. It takes only a few seconds to make an entry and review the ratings of others. Yet it provides a service that many employees will appreciate and it may help them save a few bucks by avoiding a film they wouldn't enjoy.

Many of the fun ideas I am listing can actually serve to increase attendance and reduce absenteeism. For example, one day I heard an employee say "I really felt a little under the weather today and thought about just taking the day off. But I'm going to the movies tonight and wanted to come in and check the chart before I decide what to see."

Now the movie chart is a very minor idea, I admit. But the more of these fun elements an organization can utilize, the more enjoyable the work environment becomes. And many employees have borderline days (when you feel a little less than perfect but still able to work). The more enjoyable the work environment is, the greater the likelihood that employees will decide to come to work rather than calling in sick on these borderline days.

In addition to movie charts, you might want to consider music charts (to rate the new albums), restaurant charts, book charts (to rate the new books) or theater charts (to rate the new plays) if a sizable number of your employees enjoy any of these activities.

"If Trend-Dec, Inc., will propose a two-for-one split, knock three times."

Fun Idea Number 14

Competitions for Small Prizes

Many traditionalist managers will tell you that your salary is the only reward you need for doing a good job. However, more progressive managers know that positive feedback is the most powerful motivating force at the manager's command. A good manager is constantly looking for ways to provide positive feedback to employees who do an especially good job or who meet an important goal or quota.

It's great to receive additional money or new benefits or perks for good work. However, most organizations have a limited amount of resources available for these items. Therefore, most employers need to have other means of providing recognition and rewards for good performance. Prizes are one such option.

Some prizes are better than others. Generally, prizes shouldn't be very expensive. You don't want to make the people who didn't get a prize feel bad. Yet it must be something significant enough to make the person who receives it feel good. An effective prize will vary from one group to another.

Some managers like to make up little award posters and pass them out. Some people like these. Most people don't. I hate them. What do I do with a framed piece of paper that says "Good Job, Bob" (especially when my name is Ron) or something equally inspiring? I mean it's better than nothing, which is what most managers would give you, but I think managers need to be more creative. A "Good Job, Bob" note would be okay for some quick informal feedback. One organization uses little note cards that say "You Done Good," designed like a miniature commendation. These are good, but I'm talking here about something more formal — something people compete for and win.

Here are a few ideas: You may hate these as much as I hate meaningless little plaques. This just shows the difference of reactions among various people. The key is to find a prize that people on your staff do value and not use one that makes them want to throw up every time they see it.

How about a "Stanley Cup?" The Stanley Cup, of course, is awarded each year to the ice hockey team who wins the championship. Your office could have such a cup. (You could have a contest to name the cup or name it after yourself — a shot at organizational immortality.) And each week or month or whatever, it could be passed from one person to another depending upon which employee has achieved certain goals during that time frame.

How about an extra hour for lunch every day for a week? How about letting the winner leave two hours early on Friday afternoon? Or arrive two hours late on Monday morning? Or both?

Employees enjoy a certain amount of competition. It's a game. They don't like it when it's too serious, or too important, or the losers are humiliated. But when the game is fun, and the prize is valuable but not too valuable, then this sort of competition for a prize can work well. The winner should feel good. The losers should not feel hurt. The losers should feel motivated to play again next week and try to do better. It should be a good-natured competition. If it can't be done in that vein, then better to forget it.

Fun Idea Number 15

Employee of the Month

This idea relates to the previous one. It's an idea used by many companies. Each month an employee is selected as "Employee of the Month" based upon some special contribution. Unlike the competition for a prize idea discussed above, there's usually no specific competition and no specific criteria used to select the employee of the month — although this may vary from company to company. The employee may or may not receive a prize. Usually the employee gets his or her picture taken for the company newsletter and may have his or her name placed on some type of plaque.

If done right, the Employee of the Month award can be a fun idea and can increase morale. You might want to have specific criteria. For example, your highest producer or best sales person for the month becomes Employee of the Month. However, by doing this, you're really going back to the competition/prize idea discussed above and are just naming the "Salesperson of the Month" or whatever and not "the Employee of the Month."

Thus, this type of award usually isn't limited by a specific job type or criteria. For employee of the month, everyone should be eligible including your clerical staff, secretaries, mail room workers, etc. You may want to allow your employees to select the employee of the month winner, or at least to nominate candidates with final selection by management. This gets everyone involved in the process and increases the chances that employees throughout the entire unit (which may be a specific division or the entire organization depending upon size) are considered.

Two factors are especially important in making this idea work. The process must be seen as fair. Whenever you do not have specific, objective criteria, there is a high risk that those not selected will see the process as being unfair. The person selected each month should be of such a caliber that almost everyone says, "Yes, that was a good choice for this month." For example, in one case, a relatively unknown mail room worker saved an employee's life by performing CPR and helping until the ambulance arrived. Although this was not directly work related, the mail room worker was named "Employee of the Month," and the entire staff of the organization applauded the choice.

In another case, an employee was selected after she won the women's division of a local marathon. Her victory in the race got lots of free publicity for the company, and her selection was a very popular choice among both managers and her co-workers.

So in considering "fairness" for this award, you should not just look strictly at work performance, but at overall or special contributions. The second element to make Employee of the Month awards effective is that there should be some tangible reward in addition to the picture and publicity. Most employees will enjoy seeing their photo in the company newsletter or hanging on the office wall under the "Employee of the Month" sign, but there should be something more. Cash is always a good choice, but other special benefits and perks are also effective.

Finally, although it should go without saying, the award should be timely. I know one organization that uses the employee of the month award, but the awards run about five months behind due to the complex nomination, review, and selection process. By the time an employee gets an award, he or she and fellow co-workers have usually forgotten what it was for. This is stupid and self-defeating. If your organization can't make a selection within 30 days, forget the whole idea.

Fun Idea Number 16

Manager of the Month

Although many organizations use the Employee of the Month award, few select a "Manager of the Month." This could be because many organizations don't have any good managers. (Only joking, sort of.) Yet, managers enjoy recognition too. Managers are usually excluded from the Employee of the Month award, so they should have their own.

There are dangers involved, however. If a jerk is selected for Manager of the Month, the award becomes a joke and a subject of ridicule among employees. One reason many organizations don't like to name a manager of the month is because they don't like to acknowledge which managers are held in high regard by the organization, especially if these same highly-regarded managers are held in very low regard by the rank and file employees. This type of award can force an organization to address personnel problems, problems of style, problems of perception, problems of real goals versus stated goals, etc. which the organization may prefer to avoid — although an effective organization can't avoid these issues.

One way to approach this problem is to allow the employees to nominate or select the Manager of the Month. In this manner, the award will be less likely be perceived as a joke among employees and top management will get some valuable insights into what employees think of various managers.

Fun Idea Number 17

Parking Spot For a Week or a Month

Most organizations in major cities do not provide free parking for all employees. If free parking is available at all, it's usually just for high ranking members of management, and possibly the union president. Yet, few items are as important to employees in many locations as a good parking spot. This fact provides an important reward which can be used as an incentive.

This idea can be combined with other ideas above or used separately. For example, the Employee of the Month could be provided with a priority parking spot for the month. I know a major hotel at Lake Tahoe that does this. On the other hand, the parking spot could be a prize given to someone who wins a specific competition (most increase in sales, etc.). Or the parking spot could be given out as part of an office-wide free entry lottery so that everyone has an equal chance.

Or the criteria could change each month. One month it could be the person with the newest car, or oldest car, or smallest car, or largest car, or prettiest car, or reddest car, etc. There are millions of variations. If your office has priority parking spaces, this is an idea that should definitely be considered in one form or another.

Fun Idea Number 18

Free Coffee for a Week or a Month

What is the first thing most people do as soon as they get to work? In most places, they go for coffee (decaf, hopefully), so this too becomes an item that can be used for fun and as an incentive. It too can be combined with other ideas, such as Employee of the Month, or used as a separate prize for a competition or lottery.

This can even be used as a group prize. If you have several units of a dozen or so people in each, you can select a "Unit of the Month" and provide free coffee for the whole group. You can also include donuts, cookies, or pastries if you like.

Fun Idea Number 19

Rate the Manager

This is a way to have some fun and get some valuable information. Managers frequently get to rate employees, for promotions, awards, performance appraisals, etc. Yet employees seldom get to rate their managers. It is frequently difficult for higher level managers to know what employees really think of specific managers. Here is a way to find out and let employees have some fun in the process.

The organization should design a form for employees to rate their managers. The form should have space for remarks in addition to the standard questions. At least once a year, employees should be allowed to rate their managers. This rating should focus primarily upon their first-line supervisors but shouldn't be limited to just the immediate supervisors. Employees should be able to provide input on what they think about all levels including middle and top management.

I once worked in an office in New York City which used this technique and it was extremely effective. Employees loved it. They truly enjoyed reversing the tables and rating their managers. In addition, top management got valuable information about what employees thought of all levels of management. This process helped to identify real problems which needed correcting as well as perceptual problems.

Although employees had fun doing these reviews, they also took it seriously. Out of over two thousand employees in this office, there would be less than half a dozen who would write clearly stupid or obscene types of remarks. Most employees gave the review serious consideration and provided objective, reasonable input that was of great value to the organization and the manager.

The first year it was used, managers were somewhat apprehensive, but once they saw the thoughtful nature of the comments and the reasonable manner in which employees approached it, they supported the process. Surprisingly, most managers were rated higher by their employees than they had expected. Many managers felt employees would use the review process to take cheap shots and make unfounded accusations. Yet only a tiny fraction of employees abused the process in this manner. Many managers learned important information about themselves and discovered areas where they needed to make greater efforts, especially involving employee relations.

Fun Idea Number 20

Do a Morale Survey

This idea and the next two are very important. They offer three key elements to create a positive work environment. The ideas themselves are not directly fun-oriented, but are designed to generate numerous fun ideas and other practical ideas as well. Simply put, ask your employees what they like about your organization, what they don't like, what they would like to see changed, and give them an opportunity to provide ideas and suggestions. Fun ideas should be one part of the survey, but the survey should focus on all aspects of the work environment including actual operation of the business.

Even the best managers in the world can't read minds. They don't know exactly what their employees want. Fortunately, there is a simple and direct way to find out what is on your employees' minds — ask them. This can be done using a group meeting, individual meetings, or best of all, a confidential written survey.

Designing a questionnaire is an art. However, even a poorly-designed survey is better than no survey. You may need to do some trial and error and follow-up surveys. But if you persist, you'll probably get some valuable information, including ideas for increasing fun, increasing morale, increasing quality, and increasing productivity.

Once you have a good questionnaire or survey format, you should repeat the process periodically — at least once a year and possibly more often, especially in the beginning. The survey will give you feedback on how ideas you have implemented are working and also provide a vital source of new ideas.

Of course, it's essential that you act upon the ideas. This doesn't mean that your have to implement everything suggested. You will get lots of half baked ideas and some very counterproductive and unrealistic ones. However, a substantial number of them will be good and should be implemented, at least on a trial basis.

By doing annual surveys, you'll have solid data to monitor the ups and downs of employee morale over time and get indications of causes, problems and possible solutions. You'll be light years ahead of organizations that don't care about employee morale and organizations that base their decisions on speculation about what their employees are thinking. You'll know what employees think about various issues and what they think should be done.

You won't need to be a mind reader. You can act based upon reliable information and first-hand recommendations and suggestions. I believe that any organization that doesn't do periodic surveys of employee morale doesn't really care about employee morale. And if an organization doesn't care about its employees, its employees are unlikely to care about the organization. The result is sometimes even a quick trip to Bankruptcyville.

Fun Idea Number 21

A Morale Committee

This is another important idea that builds on the morale survey. While the formal annual surveys are important, good ideas come up all the time and there is no reason to wait for a year to get them. In addition, ideas that would never even exist can be created through morale committees that engage in brainstorming sessions to generate new ideas. These committees could be called "fun committees" if their sole purpose was to generate "fun" ideas, but fun ideas are generally only a part of the process.

Almost every organization would be well-served by the establishment of morale committees. Large organizations may need dozens of such committees at various levels. There are several ways to approach the committees and different approaches will be required for different types of organizations. The committees could parallel so-called "quality circles" which deal with day-to-day work situations or they could be a distinctly separate entity which deals less with operational work flow and more with personnel policies and employee-relations issues.

The committees could be composed of both employees and managers (and union representatives in a unionized work unit) or there could be separate committees for managers and employees. Some trial and error may be needed to find the best approach in your organization. Sometimes if managers are in a group, this will inhibit employees. Likewise, managers may feel the focus is only on employee issues and not issues related to the morale of line managers and prefer a separate committee.

Whatever the composition, one of the most effective techniques for the group to use is "brainstorming." Here the group simply tries to generate as many ideas as possible without evaluating them. Evaluation can be a separate process or left to higher level managers. The purpose of the committees is not to make decisions but to generate ideas and possibly make recommendations.

Here's an example of a specific technique I sometimes use: I get a group of people together in a room, divide them into small groups of three or four, give them some general subject matter, i.e. fun ideas or ways to improve quality. I ask each group or "table" to generate as many ideas as they can and write them on notecards. The sole objective at this point is quantity of ideas, not viable ideas.

I collect the cards, give a prize to the group with the most ideas, and then start listing the ideas on poster paper attached to the walls in the room. As I list the ideas, the whole group now starts to work together. Ideas are combined and modified. Soon, the group generates several more ideas.

It's only later, sometimes even days later, that the same group or another group of employees or higher level managers review the ideas and tries to identify the viable ones. Many ideas which at first seem totally bizarre and completely impractical evolve into brilliant and practical concepts with some analysis and development.

A quote that I frequently use to initiate a brainstorming session comes from Alfred North Whitehead, the noted philosopher and mathematician, who said, "Almost all really new ideas have a certain aspect of foolishness when they are first perceived."

In an information-age work environment, ideas are valuable building blocks. These committees will give you many blocks with which to play.

Fun Idea Number 22

A Morale Manager

This is the third of the fundamental ideas for creating a positive work environment. This idea follows the morale survey and the morale committees. It involves designating a specific management official as a "morale manager" or if you prefer the mumbo-jumbo of most organizational job titles refer to it as a "motivational analyst" position. Whatever you call it, the idea is to empower someone whose primary responsibility is employee morale.

This could be the person who designs and runs your morale surveys or the one who sets up, monitors and works with your morale committees. But beyond this, the person should constantly review personnel policies and practices — including those currently in effect — and all proposed changes and modifications, with an eye towards their impact on employee morale. In sum, this person would be an employee advocate within top management.

This is not to say this person would have veto power over policies and changes. Sometimes it's necessary to do things that are unpopular. But at least this creates a process whereby employee morale becomes a major consideration in the decision-making process. You could argue that every manager should be a morale manager concerned with the impact of decisions on employee morale. This is true. But the real world seldom works this way. Many managers lose sight of employee morale in the haste of day-to-day decision making. By creating a position within top management whose primary and almost exclusive concern is employee morale, an organization can be sure that morale-related issues and concerns receive their proper consideration.

This is the same rationale that many organizations use in establishing Equal Employment Opportunity (EEO) managers and Affirmative Action managers. Although all managers should be concerned with these issues, it's frequently necessary to have a special management official assigned to monitor and address these concerns. This makes sure that the entire organization gives these matters the attention that the law and fair play requires.

When you designate a high level official to be in charge of morale, morale will become an important consideration in the decision making process.

Fun Idea Number 23

Suggestion (Criticism) Boxes

This is another good way to get a continuous flow of information from employees. You simply put up one or more suggestion boxes where employees can drop in suggestions with or without their names. This allows all employees a chance to provide input at any time on any issue. Employees like to have this opportunity and the information is vital to top management.

I call these boxes "criticism boxes" because you'll probably get as many comments (mostly negative) as you get recommendations. This may annoy some managers, but the information is important nonetheless. Top management needs to know what employees are really concerned about. It's not feasible to do employee surveys every week or month. The suggestion boxes provide ongoing input about employees concerns. Management needs negative feedback. Middle managers are all too often just "yes-men" and "yes-women." Somewhere there must be a place for honesty and reality. This could be one such place.

This is another idea designed to get information flowing up the organization rather than just down the organization. Information by the ton flows down from the top (much of it garbage). The effective organization must design ways to get info flowing up from the bottom. This is one small step in that direction.

In our office, we put two suggestion boxes on each floor in convenient locations in the hallways so that employees may drop material in them without being seen. The executive secretary collects them every two or three days and summarizes them for all the division chiefs. Employees who sign their names get a personal reply from the Chief Executive, but in practice most of the suggestions are not signed.

"Don't we have **anyone** who took business administration?"

Fun Idea Number 24

Song Writing Contest

Lest you think my ideas are getting too serious, let's discuss something totally frivolous. How about a song writing contest? Does your organization have its own official song? You can have a contest and give a prize to the employee who writes the best song. If you already have a song, have a contest anyway. It's probably time to change the song. If you don't want a company song, you can still have a song writing contest just for the hell of it. Pick a theme and have everyone write songs about it. Or have an open contest and let people write songs about any topic whatsoever. Who knows? You may get something good enough to record.

Did you ever hear the story about how Barry Manilow got started writing songs at an office song writing contest? If so, don't believe it, but it's fun to imagine anyway.

Since it's usually much harder to create something "out of nothing," than to adapt existing material, a good way for you to get started is to simply take an existing song and rewrite the words to fit your situation.

For example, I took the wonderful Randy Newman Song "I Love L.A.," which is the official song of the city of Los Angeles, and changed the words to make it "I Love LR." I used it in one of my labor relations briefings for management. I'd share the words with you, but the theme makes fun of unions.

We once had a boss named Todd. I took the old Bob Dylan anti-war song titled "With God On Our Side," and rewrote it as an anti-management song called "With Todd On Our Side."

People often ask me how I can appear to be both anti-union and anti-management at the same time. It's easy. "Management" and the "union" are functions, not people. I believe people should relate to each other as human beings, not as social-economic roles. I am "anti" any person or organization who tries to stereotype human beings into simplistic groupings like management and union. It's the "us vs. them" mindset shared by many managers and union officials that makes me critical of both sides. By poking fun at the management and union "war mentalities" and group stereotyping, I'm really just trying to get people to deal with one another as whole humans and not as economic or organizational functions.

"Try as I may, Charles, I find it difficult to believe that you are the same Charles A. Glackman who is chairman of the board of Marcar International Incorporated."

Fun Idea Number 25

A Slogan Contest

Does your organization have a slogan? Many do. And most slogans are pretty stupid. How about having a contest to get a new one? Even if you don't have one or want one, the contest is still a fun idea. It gives you an idea of what your employees think your organization is all about. The results may startle you. You can approach it seriously or admit up front that you aren't going to use it in your advertising campaigns and just seek silly slogans that would be fun to use in-house. Sometimes even silly ideas lead to a spin off, but if not, everyone has had some fun anyway. It doesn't take much time or money and it gets people thinking about the organization, its goals, its purpose, etc.

If you don't have sufficient influence to change or create the slogan for your whole company, create a slogan for your individual work unit. One factory production line which was the worst in the company adopted the slogan, "We may be last, but this will pass." Within a month, they had climbed out of the cellar and of course, they needed a new slogan, which became, "Watch out world, we're moving up!"

My slogan at my own company (Transforming Work) is "Have Fun, Will Travel."

Fun Idea Number 26

Put on a Show

Yes, I stole this one right out of the old Judy Garland and Mickey Rooney movies. "Hey gang. I've got it. Let's put on a show!" Well why not? Someone can write a little play or skit. Someone can make up some costumes. Someone can direct. Someone can manage the stage. And several people can act. It's lot of fun and great for morale.

I've often seen skits used as part of company annual conferences or association meetings, to drive home important points or highlight critical business issues in a light-hearted way.

I know an office that puts on a play every year, and the plays are very good. It's one of the highlights of the year and employees look forward to it with great anticipation. The skits center around what's going on in the office. This office is large enough to have its own auditorium to perform the plays, but if your organization isn't that big, you can always rent a hall or obtain some free space from a local church or some other organization.

Just like with the "write a song" idea, it's often easier to parody an existing show (play, movie, or TV program) than to create something totally original.

If you're enormously creative, you may be able to create a play "out of nothing," but for most of us, it's easier to simply reshape existing material. There are advantages to each approach, but for these amateur productions, parody or adaptation of an existing format is much easier than writing a work from scratch. Trying to create something from nothing can quickly discourage your group. So until you get really good at this sort of thing, it's easier to take existing material and rewrite it to make it relevant for your company.

You'll need to be a fairly large company to do this, but it's truly a lot of fun for those organizations that try it.

DOLLARS AND NONSENSE

Equally at home in the boardroom or the bedroom.

Fun Idea Number 27

Have a Talent Contest

If you don't want to try to coordinate an entire play or show, just have a talent contest. Each contestant can do their own thing. Some people can sing. Some can dance. Some can do pantomimes. Some can play musical instruments. Some can read poetry. Some can juggle. Some can do magic. Whatever. You can do it over lunch, or perhaps on the weekend so families can attend. Employees get an opportunity to show off their talents and observe the talents of others.

In one office, these talent shows began as a small group of people in a conference room, expanded to an auditorium, and finally became so large that they had to rent a theater.

Another office turned their talent show into a spoof of the Miss America pageant, which they called the "Mr./Ms. Corporation X" pageant. The various contestants went through a series of activities including a talent segment and an interview segment. Instead of an evening gown or swimsuit portion, they held a "business suit" segment, where each of the male and female contestants paraded about in their best business attire. It was an extremely hilarious parody of beauty contests.

Fun Idea Number 28

Game Shows

Have you ever wanted to be on *Wheel of Fortune?* Or how about *Jeopardy?* Whatever type of game show appeals to you, why not organize one for your employees? Again, it can be a lunch time activity or after work or on a weekend.

Better yet, work the game into your training program. I know one company that uses the *Jeopardy* format for its training sessions. The employees love it and studies show they recall much more information than when it is presented in a straight lecture format.

For example, we had our Art Department create "sets" for both *Wheel of Fortune* and *Jeopardy*, except of course, the questions related to my training topics. Instead of categories like "English Literature" or "Natural Disasters" as you might see on the *Jeopardy* show, my categories included topics such as "Labor Relations," "Employee Relations," "Performance Standards," and "Management-made Disasters." The game show format offers a good way to transform potentially boring training topics into more lively ones.

Fun Idea Number 29

Running Games

By running games, I don't mean games that involve running. I mean games that continue over a period of time. For example, I know several people who play chess at work. They make a few moves at lunch, maybe a move over break, etc. The games run on for days, sometimes weeks. Some people do the same thing with Bridge. Some people play a continuing version of Trivial Pursuit™. All you need is space to leave the games set up from day to day and employees can take advantage of this.

You can have a running game between two departments. For example, one department can challenge another to a game of chess. Each group can have a team of people who confer to select the next move. You can have the winning group get free coffee and donuts for a week, etc.

I have the computer software versions of *Wheel of Fortune* and *Jeopardy* on my personal computer and frequently play them with my friends over lunch.

Fun Idea Number 30

Jigsaw Puzzles

Puzzles are something else I hate. I find them very boring, but many people love them. And even I will sometimes try to contribute a piece or two to a group puzzle project in the office. This is another type of running game or continuing project that can't be completed in one day.

Some groups like to get extremely large or complex puzzles and spread them out on a table. From time to time someone drifts by the table and tries to place a new piece. It may take weeks or months to complete one. But there should be no hurry. It's just something to do to relax for a few seconds for those who find this relaxing.

Personally, I just find it annoying and end up wanting to kick the table over. But others actually use the puzzles as a way to calm down, relax and re-energize. I have even seen some people come up with some really good work related ideas while standing there playing with the puzzle.

When the puzzle is finally completed, you can paste it together with puzzle glue and put it up on the office wall as a monument to office down-time.

Question: Are we having Fun yet?

Fun Idea Number 31

Charades

You may feel about charades the way I feel about jigsaw puzzles and pot-luck luncheons, but I think charades are fun. It doesn't take long to play a round. You can do it over lunch in someone's office or a conference room. Or each unit can form a team and you can have weekend competitions. After dealing with complex legal or technical issues all morning, it can be fun and relaxing to act out a few charades.

The topics can include standard charade fare such as movies, books, sports, etc. You can also use topics relating to your own company, such as "Total Quality Service" or "Quality First."

Of course, as with most of these other ideas, no one should ever be forced or intimidated into participating in something they don't enjoy. The goal is fun, not conformity. Different people enjoy different activities. Or as they used to say, different strokes for different folks — which is a good phrase to try to convey in a game of charades.

Fun Idea Number 32

Feedback on Funny Post-its

Nothing is more powerful than positive feedback. Managers must constantly be alert to ways to provide employees quick, informal positive feedback for good performance. There are several quick, easy and fun ways to do this. Zig Ziglar has developed a very small form for this purpose. The form says "I like_____because _____." Then, there is room to write in what the person did that was good. At the very bottom, the form says, "You Are a Winner!" You can buy these through Mr. Ziglar's company in Texas. (The Zig Ziglar Corporation, 3330 Earhart, Suite 204, Carrollton, Texas 75006)

You can also use the little stick-on Post-it™ type papers for this same purpose. Instead of just signing a memo and giving it back, add a brief note, "Great job." This will make people feel better and create a more positive work environment.

Lots of people are obviously using this idea these days. Initially, all the Post-its were plain yellow. Then, they started coming in different sizes and different colors. Now, they come with hundreds of different pre-printed messages at the top saying things such as, "Do this for me and I'll grant you sexual favors" and "Age and treachery will overcome youth and skill" and "Here's some more bull - - - - for you." The rapidly expanding market for these packets indicates again how much people want to find ways to inject a little humor and fun into the work environment.

Fun Idea Number 33

Put Cartoons on Your Walls

By now, you should realize how much I like cartoons. I like to see them on inter-office memos, on handouts at training sessions, and in my books. I also like to see them on my walls and other people's walls.

Some people decorate their offices to get the "power look." I decorate my office for the fun look. One way to make your office or cubicle more fun is to put cartoons on your walls. The cartoons make your office look like a fun place to visit. They also serve a useful function for many people.

For example, many managers come to my office to ask me complex legal questions about labor and employee relations. Often times I must spend several minutes researching my law books or union contract to find the answer. Five minutes seems like forever when someone is staring at you wondering why you can't find the right legal precedent. However, if you have a few hundred cartoons on your wall, as I do, this gives my visitors an opportunity to read my wall, laugh and be happy, while I find the case so I can answer their question.

Another way to accomplish the same thing, in case you want your office to maintain some semblance of business decorum, is to collect a bunch of great cartoons into an album and give it to your visitors to read. Put your cartoons into plastic looseleaf sheet protectors and assemble them into a looseleaf notebook. You can label it "Laugh While You Wait" or something like that.

The managers then leave my office, not only better informed, but happier as well. It's a win-win solution.

"Last week I'm running an electronics plant in Ohio—today I'm a holy man in Kashmir. What won't my tax lawyer think of next?"

Fun Idea Number 34

Posters

Some offices have actually banned posters. Some managers think people should burn all their posters when they graduate from college. I like posters. There are fun posters. There are sexy posters. There are cynical posters. Posters can enliven an office. I would never ban posters. Certain posters can be offensive and if you deal with the public you will have to be careful not to offend anyone.

However, within the limits of good taste, posters can do a lot to perk up an office or cubicle. You might even want to consider a poster contest to see who has the best poster. You can have multiple categories. I have a few posters on my wall and would have even more except they take up too much room and limit my cartoon collection.

Fun Idea Number 35

"Pot-shots"

This is one of my all-time favorite fun ideas. There is this genius named Ashleigh Brilliant, his real name, who writes and draws something he calls "Pot-shots." They are post-card-sized cartoons or illustrated epigrams. You can buy them in many card shops or order them directly from Brilliant Enterprises, 117 W. Valeria St., Santa Barbara, CA 93101. (Send $2 for a catalog.)

I liked them so much that I dedicated my last book, *Working and Managing In the New Age,* to Mr. Brilliant. There are two examples immediately below, 40 examples in my earlier book, and over 4,000 listed in his catalogs.

They are very useful in a variety of situations. You can put them on your wall individually or buy a special container (from Brilliant Enterprises) and make a poster containing 20 of them. I have a couple of hundred on my walls — mostly in poster formats. You can feature one particular idea each day or week by putting it right on your door where everyone sees it. They are also actual post cards, so you can mail them to people. I send them through the inter-office mail as well as the U.S. mail. I also like to buy several of the same ones and pass them out at training sessions. I use them as prizes for my staff or for people in the audience at my presentations. Everyone loves them. There are dozens of uses for these delightful, humorous, insightful cards. Have more fun, order some today.

Let me give you two examples: The first is a card I used to announce a meeting which I reluctantly had to call to straighten up a mess that grew out of a previous meeting.

The second example below is a card I like to send to my employees when they are out sick, especially if the alleged illness isn't serious and I suspect they are really playing tennis or spending a few days at the beach.

OUR MEETINGS ARE HELD
TO DISCUSS MANY PROBLEMS
WHICH WOULD NEVER ARISE
IF WE HELD FEWER MEETINGS.

DON'T GET WELL
TOO SOON

YOUR SUFFERING
IS AN INSPIRATION
TO US ALL.

Fun Idea Number 36

Joke of the Day Board

You must have a bulletin board somewhere. You probably have dozens of them. Map off some space for an area you can label "Joke of the Day." Each day (or week) put up a new joke. Members of your staff can add jokes also. Best joke each day or week wins free coffee or some other prize. Jokes can be original material, cut from newspapers and magazines, or stolen from TV programs or live comedy acts.

Here's one of my favorite lawyer jokes:

There was a farmer in Alabama who wanted to sue the Railroad for running over his prize cow. He didn't have much money and couldn't afford a large law firm to handle his case, especially since he was only seeking $1,500 in damages. So the farmer hired a brand new attorney just out of law school. The Railroad went to New Orleans and hired one of the finest, most-respected lawyers in all of the South. Several months later, the case was scheduled to go to trial. The night before the trial, the Railroad's star witness, the train engineer, died. The attorney for the Railroad became very concerned.

The next morning when he arrived at court, the older attorney went to the new attorney and offered him a deal. "Why don't we just settle this whole thing right here and now for $750 and avoid all of these legal hassles?"

The young attorney immediately agreed. The papers were drawn up and signed and the case settled. The old attorney couldn't resist taking a parting shot at his rival. He said, "Son, you have a lot to learn about being a lawyer. The only reason I agreed to settle this case was because my star witness died last night."

The young attorney said, "That's okay. The only reason we agreed to settle was because last night the cow came home."

Fun Idea Number 37

Video Exchange Program

The majority of Americans now own a video cassette recorder (VCR). If you work in an office, chances are good that 75 percent or more of the employees have a VCR. Most people have several video tapes which they've purchased or copies of interesting programs they've recorded off the air (such as all the episodes of *The Prisoner* or the episode of *Moonlighting* where the would-be-lovers finally become lovers).

So here's the idea: establish a video exchange program. Have each participating employee list the videos they have which they are willing to loan to their co-workers. Prepare a consolidated list and post it on the wall somewhere. If Joe has a copy of *Cinderella* and I would like to borrow it for my child, I just contact Joe and arrange a day. If I have a copy of *Ghostbusters* and Jane wants to borrow it, she contacts me and if all goes well, Jane invites me over so we can watch it together.

Of course, you'd need to enforce the standard video store rules, such as all tapes must be rewound before returning them, no damaged tapes, accidental erasures, etc. Also, be sure to set fair time limits for the return of the tapes.

Anyway, this is just another simple, easy idea that costs little or nothing and yet makes the work environment a little more pleasant.

Fun Idea Number 38

A Music Exchange

This is exactly the same sort of idea as the video exchange except people list their audio tapes, albums, and/or CDs which they are willing to loan. I like to borrow albums and tape my favorite songs onto audio cassettes.

Again, you would need certain rules or guidelines regarding time limits, care and handling of the items, returning all the packaging etc.

All of these rules involve good common sense, but in most offices, there is usually at least one person with no common sense. This person needs the basic facts and courtesies of life spelled out. Unfortunately, often times this person is the boss.

Fun Idea Number 39

Book Exchange

Again, the same concept which we noted above for video tapes and music applied to books. You could go one step further here and set up a library in the office. We did this in one office where I worked and ended up with a library of several thousand books.

People can exchange their favorite general-interest books, books on management and career-development, self-help, mysteries, romance, fiction, westerns, etc. In short, you can exchange any type of books where you share a common interest with someone else.

Fun Idea Number 40

Spouse Exchange

Again same concept, different item. Just wanted to see if you were paying attention, although in California some offices might really do this. Actually, the exchange concept can be applied to almost anything. How about household tools or gardening equipment? I need a rake or hoe about once a decade.

Perhaps I could borrow one from a co-worker through a tool exchange. Perhaps you need a power saw three times a century. Maybe you could borrow one through this program. How about a "pasta maker," a coffee grinder, a bread maker, or a power drill? The possibilities are endless. I won't rip you off by listing any more of them among the 101 ideas, but as you can see, there is a lot of potential here.

Fun Idea Number 41

The Baby Picture Game

This is a game they played on my wife's staff once. I thought it was very clever and stole it. Each participating employee brings in one of their old baby pictures and puts it in a box without showing it to anyone. When all the pictures are in, someone puts them all up on a board or lays them all out on a table. Each one is placed near a number or letter. Then, over the next day or so, everyone fills out a form and tries to guess who is who.

When everyone has made their entries, each employee identifies their picture. The form with the most correct answers wins the prize. This is a lot more difficult than you might think, especially with a large unit of 40 or more people. Anyone who can guess 75 percent or more is doing an excellent job.

Again, this costs virtually nothing, takes very little time, and is a lot of fun. A variation or alternative is for employees to bring in pictures of their parents (or children) and see if people can match up the correct families.

You can give prizes to the winners, ranging from something substantial, a "gag" gift, or just not even bother with prizes at all. Many of these types of games are inherently interesting and fun, so prizes are unnecessary.

Fun Idea Number 42

House Pictures

This is the same basic idea as the baby pictures. Obviously, this won't work in a small community where everyone knows where everyone else lives, but in a major metropolitan area where employees seldom, if ever, visit each others homes, this is another game you can play. Can you match me with my house?

Alternatives include photos of cars, especially in places like New York and Chicago where everyone comes to work via the train and no one ever sees your car. Another alternative is pictures of pets. Can you match Mary with her cat? Again, many variations are possible. These games are fun in and of themselves. It is nice to have prizes, but prizes are not essential.

Fun Idea Number 43

An Art Contest

What, you can't draw? Me either. But why should that stop us? It doesn't stop the kids in pre-school or kindergarten. The idea here is to have fun, not to create something that will actually hang in the Museum of Modern Art. You can draw or paint or do whatever. If the office is large enough, you may need multiple categories. If everyone is so terrible that no one could possibly "win," then turn it into a "who did it" contest and leave the artists' names off the art works (the words "art" and "artist" are used loosely here) and see if you can guess who created the various works. There may be bits of your personality in the work that even you do not see.

Fun Idea Number 44

An Essay Contest

I like to have my employees write essays on "Why I like, admire and respect my manager." In some offices, they have had even more fun with "The Thing I Hate Most About My Manager." The topics can be serious ("What I would do if I were CEO") or silly ("What I would do with a second wife/husband").

This essay idea is not as silly as it may seem. If you have a serious topic, you may get some workable ideas. Even if the subject for the essay is frivolous, you may learn a lot about people's writing skills. For example, you may realize that your secretary has fantastic writing skills that are not being fully utilized by typing and re-typing your trash all day.

You can give out prizes and read the best ones aloud at a group gathering. If they are really great, you can even try to get them published, at least in a local or company newsletter.

Fun Idea Number 45

Wham-it™

Do you ever get tense at work? Of course you do. We all do. So what do you do about it? Do you scream at your employees or boss? Do you kick the water cooler? Let's hope not. Here is a fun solution to the stress problem. It's call Wham-it™, the anti-stress device. It's like a little punching bag and it's sold in card and gift stores. It comes in many different sizes from a desk top model to a giant six-footer. When you get upset, you just give your friendly Wham-it a smash in the head. It falls over, does a few loops, and springs back begging for more.

It does wonders for your mood and is less likely to get you fired than screaming at your boss (we won't even consider actually hitting your boss). You might even have a Wham-it type device in your house right now. Many children have "bop bags" of this nature with Mickey Mouse or Donald Duck on them. If your children have one, take it. You need it worse than they do.

But Wham-its are even better than the children's versions because they are specifically designed for stress and have several explicit instructions right on them explaining how many kicks or punches you should give your Wham-it depending upon the source and magnitude of your stress.

I have had my Wham-it for three years now and I love it. I even bring it with me when I do hearings or make presentations. If some stupid arbitrator overrules my motion, I could break out into an unprofessional outburst and pound on the table. Instead, I ask for a three minute recess, step into the witness room and knock my friendly Wham-it around for 30 seconds and I'm back in control. (This also serves to keep my next witness alert.)

Get your Wham-it today. Add ten years to your life.

Fun Idea Number 46

Meet Your Team at the Airport

This has never actually happened to me, but every time I suffer through one of those eight-hour cross country flights with a plane change in Chicago, I fantasize about it. Think about this. The Oakland A's win the pennant. They fly back into town. Thousands of people meet them at the airport at 2 a.m. The New York Mets lose the playoffs. They fly back to New York. Ten thousand people meet them at Kennedy airport at 3 a.m., and they were the losers.

I want an airport greeting with hundreds of cheering fans, banners, and confetti when I return from Los Angeles after winning a hearing, or settling a labor dispute, or making a brilliant presentation at a conference. Why not?

Now, I don't expect you to meet me. But think about your own organization. How about the next time Jack or Jill lands a big contract or does something great in whatever line of business you're in, you and as many people as possible, drive out to the airport with a few placards, banners and signs and give your team (or guy or gal) a really warm greeting when they come off that plane. It's a day they'll never forget.

Maybe sometime they'll organize a reception for you after you've had a good trip. What's the worst that could happen — you waste a few hours and catch Jack traveling with his mistress and charging her on the company account, but it's a small risk to run to give your team the reception they deserve. Think about it.

Fun Idea Number 47

Cartoon of the Day

This is similar to the Joke of the Day idea. Set up a bulletin board for cartoons. Each day (or week) put up a favorite from the newspaper, magazines, or wherever. All employees can add cartoons to the collection. You could have a prize for the person to contribute the best cartoon each week. This is a great way to get lots of cartoons for your cartoon file. Here is my entry for the week.

Immediately after Orville Wright's historic 12-second flight, his luggage could not be located.

Fun Idea Number 48

Social Secretary or Morale Assistant

This is an idea for very large offices with hundreds or thousands of employees. If your office or division ends up doing several of these fun projects, you may find that you need a social secretary or a morale assistant to coordinate the fun and games. Perhaps you can find a cruise director who is ready to give up the sailing life and live on land. One of those types of people with a bubbly, cheerful, personality would be perfect.

If you really get into creating a positive work environment, you'll find that it's rather time-consuming. Someone has to coordinate the activities, make sure the right type of rooms are reserved, get the supplies and props ordered, etc. This is where a social secretary would really come in handy. It can easily become a fulltime job in a large organization. But, why not?

Fun Idea Number 49

Brainstorming Sessions for Fun Ideas

This idea can supplement or in certain cases replace Fun Idea Number 21 (the Morale Committees). Here instead of a standing committee that deals with all aspects of morale you have a one-time only brainstorming session or sessions at which all employees have an opportunity to contribute ideas and suggestions for making the office a fun place to work. These sessions almost never fail to generate at least a few good ideas.

If you're a small business, you may have a need to choose a name for a product, invent an advertising slogan, or work out a promotional gimmick for a sale. Brainstorming sessions can produce very valuable business ideas.

As I noted earlier, the purpose of brainstorming is to create the maximum number of alternatives or ideas, regardless of quality or feasibility. Many people are so self-critical that they can't develop an idea without immediately jumping all over it. These brainstorming sessions, which put off the critical or analytical process for another time (and another person), allow everyone to generate ideas without this self-imposed barrier.

Of course, someone must eventually evaluate the ideas and try to act upon them — otherwise the whole process becomes a farce. But the creativity and the critical analyses should be clearly separated.

Fun Idea Number 50

A Photography Exhibit

The average family owns something like 3.5 cameras and takes approximately 234 pictures a year. (Where does he get these amazing statistics? Yes, that's right. I make them up.) Anyway, while most of these pictures are of little Sarah sticking her tongue out at the camera, a few are actually worth seeing. Some vacation photos are especially interesting, and most offices have at least a few semi-serious photographers who do really good stuff. You may as well take advantage of all these pictures by having an office photography exhibit and encouraging all the employees to bring in their favorite photos.

Some offices like to use the photos for a lobby display. Other offices just post the photos in the individual work areas. You can have judges and prizes or you can just do it for the fun of it.

Fun Idea Number 51

Okay, Now You Do Something

We are now half way through the 101 fun ideas. While I reflect on the first 50 and tap my creativity banks for another 50, it's time for you to try your hand at this. Is one idea too much to ask? I know you will be tempted to skip ahead and read Fun Idea Number 52, but STOP.

Hey, let's make this a test of will. Think for a few minutes. Can you come up with one new idea for creating fun in your work environment that I haven't mentioned yet? There are many more ideas. In fact, I have at least 50 more that I will share with you. So the well isn't dry yet. There are many more ideas. What's yours?

Write your fun idea in this box:

My fun idea is:

Fun Idea Number 52

Buckeyes

Hey, I hope you aren't cheating. You developed at least one idea of your own, didn't you? If not, go to jail, don't pass go, don't collect $200. You can't get out free until you generate at least one fun idea.

Okay, now let's talk about "buckeyes." What are buckeyes? I don't know either, to tell you the truth. I think they're some kind of tree with chestnuts. But I know about Buckeyes thanks to Ohio State. The Ohio State football team is called "the Buckeyes." Whenever a player on the team has a good game, he is awarded a "buckeye" for his helmet. By the time a good player is a senior, he probably has several dozen buckeyes on his helmet.

Now buckeyes don't mean much of anything in and of themselves, but they represent good performance. Your office could select an appropriate symbol and give one to your employees when they have performed well. Some ideas are obvious. Apple Computers would be stupid to use anything other than an apple. Other companies may not have such a ready-made symbol. You could have a contest to develop the symbol.

Once you have the symbol, you can order thousands of them in the form of stickers or tiny knick-knacks or buttons or whatever. Whenever employees turn in good performances, give them buckeyes. They can stick them on their walls, or on their desks or on their computers. It may sound silly, but it worked for former Ohio State football coach Woody Hayes.

Fun Idea Number 53

The "Mickey Mouse" Award

Every office should have a "Mickey Mouse" award, literally. You can buy a Mickey Mouse™ stuffed doll or a Mickey Mouse picture or any of a hundred items with Mickey on them. This item then becomes your "Mickey Mouse" award. Periodically, perhaps weekly or monthly depending upon the size of your organization, you can give the award to someone for doing something which seems at first glance to be a small accomplishment but that is really symbolic of something much larger.

Now, let me first explain to you about Mickey Mouse organizations. Through some process which is unclear to me the phrase "Mickey Mouse" has taken on certain negative connotations. If a manager makes employees raise their hands and get permission to go to the rest rooms (or something almost equally silly), employees will say the manager is "Mickey Mouse" (and other names too obscene for a family book, but you get the idea). If someone said your organization was "Mickey Mouse," you would probably be insulted. But I think it is time to change this negative connotation.

In California and Florida, the best example of a "Mickey Mouse" company is Disneyland — one of the most efficient, best-managed organizations in the world.

We should all be so lucky as to work for a Mickey Mouse organization like this. So I think it is time we gave Mickey some respect and the Mickey Mouse award is a step in that direction.

Disneyland and Disney World are excellent organizations because they take care of the small things. They handle the minor details that many companies overlook or ignore. This fact forms the idea for the award. You should award the "Mickey" to someone who demonstrates a readiness to take care of the minor details. This may be someone low or high in the organization. The action should be the sort of thing that is not normally recognized by larger awards, but the sort of thing that is essential to take care of. Some examples include recognizing people who clean the office, service the photocopy machine, install toilet paper in the restrooms, deliver the inter-office mail, provide security for the office or parking lot, etc.

These activities are very important. If your photocopy machine goes down, you know you're in big trouble. Yet how often do you recognize the people who service them and keep them running. If you have public restrooms (for example, if you manage a restaurant or amusement park or any type of business where the public uses your facility) it's very important that the restrooms be cleaned and "papered" periodically throughout the day. Failure to do so will make a very unfavorable impression upon your customers. Yet, how often do you think these people who do this type of work are recognized in any positive way?

However, the award should not be limited to "the little people" or the "forgotten people" in the organization. High level managers should be considered for the "Mickey" when they take special care to make sure the seemingly small, insignificant details are covered or when they go the extra mile to maintain quality service. There are hundreds of stories about top managers pitching in and doing unexpected duties.

For example, an executive vice president of a major computer repair corporation learned that a company truck had broken down on the way to deliver a part that a customer had ordered. It would have been easy and acceptable to simply call the customer and explain that the truck broke down and delivery would be delayed one day. The customer probably wouldn't even have complained. We are all so used to delays that we accept them without complaints most of the time.

Yet, this vice president got in his car and drove 75 miles to pick up the part from the broken down truck and then drove another 120 miles to deliver the part on time.

In my opinion, he should have gotten a "Mickey Mouse" award for outstanding performance. When employees understand that "Mickey" represents excellence and going the "extra mile" to take care of all the essential details, employees will look fondly upon the award and be proud to be known as winners of the "Mickey Mouse" award. If your company has big bucks, throw in a free trip to Disneyland for the winner and employees will appreciate the award even more.

Welcome to 'You're Fired.' My first guest is an employee whose brand of fun-loving incompetence has been a delight to everyone in the company but me.

Fun Idea Number 54

Weight Loss Contest

You must be very careful to suggest this idea. If you're a tall, thin person who eats chocolate bars all day and never gains a pound, don't even think of suggesting this to your flabby co-workers. But if you have gone beyond pleasantly plump and are often mistaken for the Pillsbury Dough Boy, it may be safe for you to suggest this idea.

One of the disadvantages of working in an office is that we get very little exercise. In addition, it's tempting to nibble all day long on one type of goodie or another (chips and chocolate are my weaknesses). Thus, it's very easy to gain weight. One way to lose weight, improve your health and have some fun is to organize a weight reduction group at work and have weekly weigh-ins. You can have a variety of prizes to motivate people.

I once worked in an office where the average employee was about 50 pounds overweight. It was disgusting. If there were more than two people on an elevator, you'd have to wait until the next one came along. I didn't dare suggest this idea of a weight reducing club to them being a thin person myself, but eventually they did organize such a group. They had a lot of fun and lost enough weight that our electricity bill for the elevators actually went down!

Fun Idea Number 55

A Poetry Reading

Each employee selects one of his or her favorite poems. It could be something serious (T. S. Eliot or William Blake) or something from Mother Goose. Some day over lunch, you gather together and take turns reading your poems to each other. There are hundreds of poems that I enjoy, but being an incurable romantic, my very favorites deal with love. One of my favorite favorites goes as follows:

Love's Philosophy

The foundations mingle with the river
    And the rivers with the ocean;
The winds of heaven mix forever
    With a sweet emotion;
Nothing in the world is single;
    All things by a law divine
In one another's being mingle —
    Why not I with thine?
See the mountains kiss high heaven,
    And the waves clasp one another;
No sister-flower would be forgiven
    If it disdain'd its brother:
And the sunlight clasps the earth,
    And the moonbeams kiss the sea —
What are all these kissings worth,
    If thou kiss not me?

Percy Bysshe Shelley (1792-1822)

I've heard that this poem has been used in more successful seductions than any other poem in the history of the English-speaking world. Perhaps you should memorize it.

Fun Idea Number 56

A Hot Tub Party

Yes, I know what you're thinking, "That's so California!" But fun is fun and Californians understand hedonism like few people in the world. That is why hot tubbing is so popular in the Golden State. You'll probably need to have your hot tub party after work at someone's house or at one of those hot tub rental establishments. An advantage of the rental places is that they have really big tubs and Jacuzzis™ that can accommodate large groups. However, if your company is truly progressive and out there on the cutting edge of the future, then the office should have its own hot tub where employees can go soak when they need to relax and unwind.

A question that inevitably comes up when discussing hot tubbing is, "Do I have to take my clothes off?" Would you take a regular bath with your clothes on? Do you shower with your clothes on? Seriously, the best way to hot tub is sans clothes. However, most people are modest, especially around their co-workers. And getting all your employees together in a tub, naked, could lead to some sexual harassment litigation. So it is acceptable to have a party with people in swim suits.

If hot tubbing seems too "California" for you, then just have a swim party at the pool.

Fun Idea Number 57

A "Bargain" Board

Some people would rather shop than eat. Some people get more turned on by "sales" than they do by sex. Some people would rather buy a $300 suit at half price than buy the same suit at the regular price of $140. Some people can't resist a bargain — or at least something labeled as a bargain. (Some people are seriously twisted in the head.) And some of these people work for you. Let them have a little fun.

Put up a bulletin board for "sales." Whenever someone sees a big sale advertised in the newspaper, they can cut out the ad and place it on the board and share the exciting news with all their bargain hunting friends. The Board can also be used to put up the ads we all get in our mail every day or just to put up handwritten notes. No one ever need miss out on a "sale" again. You can call your board the "Bargain Board."

You can post it in the hallway and you can put one of you unit's top "bargain hunters" in charge of taking care of it.

Fun Idea Number 58

Hold Your Meetings Outdoors

Some people like meetings. These people are really, Really, RE-ALLY twisted. Other people would rather be beaten by a stick than spend an hour in a meeting. Yet meetings are a way of life in most organizations. Can anything be done to make meetings more tolerable? Yes, of course. I wouldn't have asked the question if I didn't have the answer. Several things can be done. Some of which we have already listed. Jokes, stories and entertainment, cartoons on handouts, etc.

But here's another idea to make meetings better: hold them outdoors whenever possible. I'm not talking about January in Chicago or August in New Orleans. But in most places, there are many days, especially in the spring and fall, when it's very pleasant outdoors. My office has a large patio area which is perfect for outdoor meetings. If you don't have anything similar to this, consider using a nearby park. There's something wonderfully refreshing about being outdoors when the weather is nice that even a meeting can't totally destroy.

Besides it's great fun to watch the look of panic on your boss's face when the notes for his or her two-hour speech get blown away in the wind. Seriously, meeting outdoors does require a little preparation. I've held many meetings on our outdoor patio. One of the first things I do is put sun block on my nose. Otherwise, the next day I look like Rudolph. Then, I bring a paper weight in my brief case to hold my papers down and keep them from blowing away. Depending upon the time and place where you're meeting, there may be a few other minor preparations you'll need to make, but it's worth it. Meeting outside is a dramatic improvement over the big formal conference room. You can even hold seminars and training sessions outside.

DOLLAR$ AND NONENE

Well, I've got an office and I've got a window, but I wouldn't say I've got a window office.

Fun Idea Number 59

Have a Conference at the Beach

Once you get used to meeting outdoors, you'll start to look for ways to get further and further from the office. If you're lucky enough to live near a beach, you have a perfect setting. Unless your office is right on the beach, it probably won't be practical to have everyone drive to the beach for a regular meeting (in their suits and business dresses). But if you have a full-day conference, then the beach idea is more practical.

Everyone can dress accordingly and meet at the beach. You'll need to bring some folding tables and beach chairs so people can sit and work comfortably. Two especially vital items are sun block for your face and a clipboard for your papers. Otherwise, the sun will beat down on you and the wind will blow everything away and you'll spend the afternoon, literally, on a "paper chase."

Would you believe that the managers at General Motors got the idea for the joint project with Toyota at a beach conference? I don't either. But beach conferences are an interesting idea anyway.

If you don't live near a beach, then move. Seriously, other good alternatives are a conference at the pool club or in the park.

Fun Idea Number 60

Have Your Meetings in a Private Home

Here's one more idea for off-site meetings. My wife's staff used to do this: They would hold their quarterly planning conferences in the homes of one of the staff members. The site would rotate each quarter. There would be lots of food and drinks. When the weather was good, they could move out to the decks or patios. It didn't cost anything in terms of rental fees. Everyone had a lot of fun and, amazingly, they got a lot of work done.

Fun Idea Number 61

What's My Favorite TV Show?

This is another game to play with your staff. Make a list with everyone's name on it. Each employee gets a copy. Everyone tries to guess the favorite TV show of the other staff members. Eliminate news and sports programs. When everyone has made their guesses, each employee tells his or her favorite to the group. The individual with the most correct answers wins the prize. Did you guess *thirtysomething* for me? If so, you're right.

Fun Idea Number 62

What's My Favorite Book?

This is a variation on the TV game before. Here each employee tries to guess the favorite book of the other staff members. This is actually a very difficult question to answer. I have about a hundred favorites. So it may make it easier to break this down into categories such as fiction, philosophy, politics, etc.

There are dozens of variations on this type of game. You can ask the same "What's Your Favorite . . ." question on a large number of topics including movies, plays, etc.

Another purpose for all of these games is to promote social cohesion among the workers in your unit. It's often amazing to realize how little we actually know about our co-workers. They exist as "functions" or "roles," but not as real human beings.. Games such as these give employees an opportunity to relate to each other as people.

Fun Idea Number 63

Awards Ceremony

This is something else that I hate but many people love. One of my first assignments when I went to work in the area of employee relations was to organize an awards ceremony to recognize several hundred employees who received an award over the previous year for either excellent performance or length of service with the organization. I didn't feel this was a proper use of my valuable time and almost quit.

But I went ahead and put it together, marching bands, flag teams, a 50-piece orchestra, etc. I thought it was the silliest thing I had ever seen, but the employees loved it. They invited their families to come. They took pictures. It was like high school graduation all over again.

This was an important lesson to me and should be an important lesson for you too. Just because I (you) don't like something doesn't mean beans. The question you should ask yourself is, "Do the people you are recognizing like it?" If the answer is a solid "yes," then you should go ahead with the plans.

Fun Idea Number 64

The Personal Dart Board

Have a dart board made with the boss's picture on it. When employees get ticked at the boss, they can throw darts at him or her to let off steam rather than engaging in more destructive acts, such as unleashing a computer virus.

Several variations are possible. One of the most common is the punching bag with the boss's face on it. This is used by several companies in Japan. When the employees get upset, they go into a special sound proof room, get a stick or club, and pound away at this big bag that looks just like the boss.

This reduces stress, relieves anxiety, and helps the employees feel better. Besides, it's better that they beat up on the bag than the actual boss.

Fun Idea Number 65

Take A Cruise

This requires some REAL money. Cruising is expensive, but it's also a very relaxing way to travel. More and more business and management conferences are being held aboard cruise ships. There are several ways to take advantages of cruising. One is to send your managers to a conference scheduled on a cruise ship. Another is to send your top managers or award-winning employees on a cruise together and have meetings, seminars and workshops designed specifically for your staff as part of the cruise package. Sometimes you can find an economical one-day cruise.

Lastly, you can discard any pretense of working on the cruise and send your award-winning employees and managers on a cruise strictly for relaxation.

If the organization can't afford any of these alternatives, then the managers and employees of the organization may still want to consider vacationing together on a cruise and paying for it themselves. One advantage to this approach is that if you can put a group together, you can usually get a substantial discount from the cruise line.

A final idea is to simply rent a medium sized sail boat for a day and have a floating conference or meeting.

Fun Idea Number 66

Send Your Employees to a Comedy Writing Workshop

There has been a dramatic increase in comedy workshops over the past few years. One of the reasons for this is that many managers, employees and companies understand the importance of injecting humor into workplace presentations. Managers and employees are signing up for comedy workshops on their own and many companies are paying to send their managers to these comedy workshops. If you don't think your managers or employees are funny enough, send them to a class.

An instructor, usually a fairly well-known comedy writer, will teach your employees the basic steps of comedy writing. Like everything else, there are tricks which make comedy easier to create. These classes vary in length from a one-day workshop to a full seminar. After the session, your managers should have a greater ability to find humor in various situations and share that humorous perception with others.

Fun Idea Number 67

Have Branches of Social Organizations On-Site

In my office we have several social organizations that hold meetings at lunch and breaks. For example, we have our own Toastmasters Club to give our employees experience in public speaking. We have our own "Overeaters Anonymous" to coordinate weight control programs. There are numerous other possibilities. Activities that are primarily for the benefit of the employees are off-the-clock and on the employees' own time. Activities that have reasonably direct benefits to the organization (such as Toastmasters) are usually split 50/50. The meetings are usually held in a conference room and publicized in the company newsletter.

Fun Idea Number 68

Start the Day with a Sing-a-Long

You'll need to have a real fun loving group to try this. Many employees think they are too sophisticated for something of this nature. It may also be a bit much to do it every day. You might want to consider just doing it on Monday mornings when everyone needs a special lift to get going.

Simply get your staff together and sing the company song (or any other happy or work song) at the beginning of the day. Some good choices are "Life Is So Good" by John Denver, "Maggie's Farm" by Bob Dylan, or "The Work Song" by Maria Muldaur.

You can give each employee a handout with the words to the songs and gather by the boss's desk on Monday mornings. I wouldn't do this in front of the building where the general public can see you — they might think you're totally bananas!

Fun Idea Number 69

Free Coffee and Donuts on Mondays

Want to do something to jump-start the week that is a little less silly than having a Sing-a-Long? Provide free coffee and donuts to the staff every Monday morning. Mondays are tough. Mondays are a high absentee day. Even many employees who make it in on Mondays are a little on the tardy side. Having free coffee and donuts (or orange juice and bagels or whatever) may be just enough to motivate the staff to make the effort to get in on time and take advantage of these freebies.

Fun Idea Number 70

Have a Dance

This is another after-hours activity. Invite all your employees and their spouses, significant others, or dates to a dance. There is a theory that these socials events help to build team spirit, loyalty, group cohesion, etc. There is an opposing theory to the effect that these events breed conflict, adultery, jealousy, etc. Which theory is correct? Who knows? But either way, you'll have a lot of fun.

GOOD NEWS/BAD NEWS

Gentlemen, I'd like to close this meeting with a short prayer: Lord, let us get away with this little scheme just this once. Amen.

Fun Idea Number 71

Have a Silly Song Contest

This is, by definition, a silly idea. Each employee brings in a recording or tape of his or her favorite silly song. At lunch, the songs are played for the group. The person with the silliest song wins. Here are a few past winners of silly song contests, "On the Amazon" by Don McLean, "Dirty Laundry" and "Johnny Can't Read" by Don Henley, and of course that classic "A Silly Song" from Snow White and the Seven Dwarfs.

GOOD NEWS/BAD NEWS

I think the signing of contracts calls for a toast, don't you?

Fun Idea Number 72

Have a Stand-up Comedy Contest

After you've sent your staff to the comedy workshops, you might as well see the results. Have a stand-up comedy contest. Each employee gets to do a five minute routine. Do it over lunch or have it after work at a local club. Invite friends and family. Who knows? This could be the launching of the next Woody Allen or Eddie Murphy.

Fun Idea Number 73

The Millionth Fan Award

Baseball teams frequently give an award to the fan who happens to walk through the turnstiles and become the millionth fan to attend a game that year. This same concept can be applied to many activities. If you produce cars, shoes, or if your office approves loans, claims, or whatever, the idea is the same. Pick an important number. The employee who just happens to produce or handle that item gets a special award. It's pure luck, but this gives everyone a chance and keeps everyone interested.

To show you how this idea can be used in a very twisted kind of way, let me give you a really fun example. I've mentioned that I used to manage an employee relations staff. One of our many functions was helping operations' managers fire incompetent employees. Now we took reasonable steps to help employees improve and get back on track, but if they failed to improve over a period of some months, there was no choice but to fire them. So I set the magic number at 25. The person on my staff who happened to handle the case to fire the 25th person in any fiscal year got an award. We called it the "Hatchet Man" award. The winner got a plastic axe to put on his or her office wall and free coffee and doughnuts for a week. When you are in the unpleasant business of firing people, you need lots of silly ideas to keep people in a positive mood.

Fun Idea Number 74

Have a Cynical Song Contest

Some of my favorite songs are of the cynical variety. I especially like early Bob Dylan. I find a great deal of fun in being cynical. But cynicism must be handled correctly. It can't become too bitter or too serious. I consider myself somewhat of an expert on "balanced cynicism" or cynicism which is fun, but not too negative or bitter. I even have a segment in one of my workshops called "enlightened cynicism" which tries to teach this thought process.

The cynical song contest is similar to the silly song contest except each staff member brings in his or her favorite cynical song. Past winners have included "It's All Right Ma, I'm Only Bleeding" by Bob Dylan and "Working Class Hero" by John Lennon.

Fun Idea Number 75

Make "Fun" an Appraisal Item on the Annual Performance Review

One way to make sure everyone in the organization is doing everything they can to create a "fun" work environment is to have an item in your annual performance ratings on fun. Just like you rate managers and employees on how well they perform various work and production aspects of their jobs, you can also rate them on how well they created a fun work environment.

This is an indirect way to generate a lot of fun activities for your organization.

You could have an appraisal item called "Promotes A Creative Work Environment" and rate managers on their ability to do so. One good way to get valuable feedback from employees on such an evaluation is with an annual employee survey or a "Rate the Manager" approach.

Fun Idea Number 76

Recruit Fun People

Probably no idea on the list is more effective than this one. If you start with fun people, you will have a fun work environment. If you start with people who are clinically depressed, the work environment isn't going to be much fun no matter how many clever ideas you develop.

For a period of time I worked in a division where 80 percent of the employees were clinically depressed. If I tried to do anything to cheer them up, they would try to kill me. They didn't want to have any fun. They were fully committed to being depressed and didn't want anyone or anything trying to bring them out of it. The only time I ever saw many of them smile was once when one of their co-workers died of AIDS. These people were seriously warped. I finally had to give up and admit that even I (Mr. Sunshine) couldn't get these people to have fun.

Therefore, if you want to have a fun office, recruit fun people. Recognize there are limits to what you can do to change people. Include an element in your recruitment testing to determine if job applicants are likely to be positively oriented to fun. Give them a smile test, a laugh test and have them tell jokes during their interviews. If they can't smile, laugh and tell jokes, burn their applications. You don't need people who can't laugh and smile.

By the way, this is the way a "smile test" works: When you are interviewing a job applicant, you simply say, "I want to test your ability to smile. I will count to three and then we will both flash a smile and hold it for five seconds. One, two, three, smile!" You then smile broadly at the applicant. If the applicant smiles back, he or she passes the test. If the applicant fails to smile, he or she fails. You then do the "laugh test" the same way, except you laugh aloud rather than just smiling. If the applicants pass both the smile and laugh tests, then ask them to tell you their favorite joke. If they can't think of a joke, say, "Don't call us. We'll call you." If they tell you a good joke, say, "We'll be getting back to you." If they say, "I have so many good jokes I'm not sure which one to use" and proceed to tell you three good jokes, just say "When can you start?"

Yes, yes, I know. It's not that simple. But it is important to have screening devices to weed out the lemon brains. Another option is to add a question to your job application which asks, "Do you think work should be fun?" If they answer "no," then you can have all the fun of telling them to go look elsewhere for a job.

Fun Idea Number 77

Create a Fun Waiting Area

This idea is primarily directed at your clients and customers and only indirectly at your employees. However, it will have very positive implications for your employees as well. If you have a business where people come into your office to meet with you and your employees and they have to spend more than one minute in a waiting area, then consider this idea.

People hate to wait. Waiting puts them in a bad mood. They will then take their bad mood out on you, your employees and your organization. You may well lose their business entirely. Yet, it's virtually impossible to coordinate activities in such a way to eliminate all waiting.

The idea is to make waiting as pleasant as possible and try to use this inevitable waiting time to get your customers into a good mood rather than allowing them to sink into a bad mood. Of course, doctors and dentists and accountants and lawyers have used magazines for years for this purpose. But magazines don't accomplish anything positive. If the wait is brief, a magazine may help prevent the customer from sinking into a bad mood, but if the wait gets too long, the customers will likely throw the magazine across the room (or at least feel like it).

We want to accomplish something positive with our waiting time, not just minimize the negative impact. There are many ways to approach this and the way you choose will depend primarily upon what type of clients you have. Here is one idea. Install a TV/ VCR combination in the waiting area and play various "up" or "fun" programs.

If you service a youth oriented clientele, play rock videos. If you service an older group, play comedy programs (perhaps tapes of *I Love Lucy*). If you service children, play cartoons. If you are a travel company, play vacation videos. If you service elderly people from the radio era, have an audio tape playing some of the famous old comedy routines from "radio days." Get the idea?

By doing something positive with this waiting time, the customers will be in a better mood. They will treat you and your employees nicely and this will help everyone have a more enjoyable day. They'll also be more likely to look positively upon your organization and do business with you again. It's a win/win/win proposition which costs you very little and pays high dividends.

One final note on this point. Never make people wait in a line if there is any way to avoid it. Let people take a number, sit and rest, and be called when it's their turn. It may make sense to wait in a line at McDonald's, but it doesn't make sense to wait in a line at most professional organizations, such as banks.

Fun Idea Number 78

Show Video Movies Over Lunch

If you have a TV and VCR in your office, you can show videos over lunch. Employees can bring in their favorite videos from home or they can rent them at a video store. They may want to see "home videos" of vacations and other events as well as professional videos. If they plan to watch a regular movie, they may need to show it over a two or three day period depending upon the length of the movie and the length of the lunch period. You can kick this off with by showing the movie *How to Succeed in Business Without Really Trying*.

Another approach we have used is to check out free videos from the local library. We've borrowed *The History of Civilization, Art In the Western World* and others. You can also show educational or self-development videos that help people work better, if the subjects are interesting enough.

Fun Idea Number 79

Have a Picnic at Lunch

If you're near a park (even one of those little "city parks"), you can have a picnic over lunch some day. What could be more fun than spending your lunch period with your employees and a million ants? This is another one of those ideas that I probably wouldn't do since I don't like picnics, but my wife's staff does this from time to time and everyone really enjoys it.

If you're lucky enough to have a park within walking distance, this is a real snap. Otherwise, you'll need to organize some carpools. Have everyone bring a blanket and a brown bag lunch. Also bring at least one highly-dedicated employee to keep track of the time so you don't all get fired.

Fun Idea Number 80

Have Outside Speakers/Entertainers Over Lunch

You'll probably need a big office for this. We have a 600-seat auditorium in our office which is perfect for this sort of thing. You can invite in speakers on a wide variety of issues from AIDS to avoiding colds, to handling child care problems, to planning for retirement, to various business and career related topics. In addition, you can go beyond standard speakers and bring in entertainers to sing, dance, do magic, tell jokes, etc.

We've had everyone from the local Congresswoman to the San Francisco 49er's Cheerleaders. We've had marching bands, orchestras, string quartets, country music singers, and jazz groups. We've had Polynesian dancers and ballet. We had a "feminist" comedian who left the audience rolling in the floor with laughter and we had a survivor of the Nazi death camps who left the audience in tears and with a much better understanding of the evils of discrimination and prejudice.

The possibilities are endless. Whether the program is educational or strictly entertainment, employees will appreciate the opportunity to laugh or learn over their lunch periods. We call them "brown bag presentations" because most of the employees bring a quick lunch with them to eat while they watch the presentation.

Fun Idea Number 81

Rookie of the Year

There are several sports awards that can be ripped off and used in the office or work environment. One of my favorites is "Rookie of the Year." This involves the selection of the new employee who has done the most to help the organization over the past year. You can also have "Manager of the Year" and "Rookie Manager of the Year" and "Comeback of the Year" awards. You can select a "Most Valuable Player" in each division. You can have a "Cy Young Award" for the most valuable person in a particular job type that is especially vital for the organization. You can have "Player of the Game" awards for individuals who were especially helpful with a specific project.

Use your imagination and you can probably think of dozens of these awards you could use in your organization. If your organization has big bucks, perhaps you can give World Series tickets to the award winners. Or if the winners aren't sports fans, give them tickets to the opera or whatever they would appreciate.

Fun Idea Number 82

Crossword Puzzles

Normally, I would just as soon watch a mime perform as do a crossword puzzle (which is to say, BORING). However, there are a couple of situations where I find crosswords tolerable. Both of these situations can apply to the work environment. The first is the group puzzle. You get a very large crossword puzzle. You put it up on a wall or perhaps lay it on a table. The entire staff works on it. You don't try to do it all in one day. But from time to time, when you need a mini-break, you walk over to the puzzle and take a shot at a word. It may take weeks or months to complete the puzzle, but there's no rush.

You can get giant-sized puzzles at many card shops or you can have your art department (or a college art department) create one for you with special questions designed for your organization. You can also use photocopies to enlarge it with successive copies.

The second interesting way to use crossword puzzles is to post them on the side walls of the rest room stalls so that employees have something to do while they sit and wait for nature to take its course. It's better than having employees write obscenities on the walls and they may even learn something.

Fun Idea Number 83

Give This Book to All Your Employees

This is a self-serving idea. I admit it. But I think it's a good idea nonetheless. I've written a number of books, two of which relate directly to work and management. One, of course, is this delightful book that you're now holding. It makes a fun and helpful gift for many of your employees and managers. The books could even be used as prizes for some of the various quizzes, contests and awards I have listed. Don't dismiss this idea just because it would make me and my publisher some money.

"Let me just make a little note of that. I never seem to get anything done around here unless I make little notes."

Fun Idea Number 84

A Limo for a Day or a Week

Most of us commute to work. A few top executives get free limo service as part of their jobs, but this is very rare. Here's an idea for a great prize or award for one of your employees who has done something noteworthy to help your business.

Hire a chauffeur to have a limousine to pick the employee up at his or her home and drive him or her to work and back each day for a week. The limo should be top of the line with a TV, bar (for after work use only), stereo, etc. This is the kind of extravagance that few, if any, employees would ever do for themselves. Thus, it becomes a most unusual prize or award that they will never forget.

Fun Idea Number 85

Computer Generated Jokes

This is an idea for an organization that has several employees who work much of the day at computer terminals. There is a company called Enlighten in Michigan who has developed a software program called "Chuckle Pops" that allows computer users to call up a series of jokes while they work. Other similar programs can't be far behind.

With one of these programs in your system, your employees can periodically call up a joke to break the dull routine of keying data. Or if the program is really sophisticated, the program can itself generate a joke every 30 to 60 minutes by displaying a flashing symbol to alert the computer user to the fact that a joke is waiting to be displayed at their next convenient breaking point.

Question: What's the Official Flower of the Labor Relations Society?

Answer: The Hedge

Fun Idea Number 86

Buy Entertaining Calendars

Many organizations buy calendars for their employees to use throughout the year. Some are desk calendars. Some are wall calendars. Some are little wallet-size calendars to carry around. But almost all of these calendars are nothing more than calendars. Would you give one of these calendars to your friends for a Christmas present? I should hope not.

This should be your guide. Don't give your employees a calendar that you wouldn't give to a friend for a present. There are literally hundreds and thousands of wonderful calendars on the market. The Sierra Club has a beautiful series of calendars with photographs. There are calendars with a wide variety of themes and jokes. There is a "Far Side" calendar with some of the best of Gary Larson. Why buy a regular calendar when for only a few dollars more, you can buy something that does more than just tell you what day it is? These calendars actually help you have a nice day. This is another inexpensive way to bring a little bit of pleasure and enjoyment into your work environment.

Question: What's the Official Bumper Sticker of the Labor Relations Society?

Answer: Labor Relations Specialists Do It At The Table.

Fun Idea Number 87

Have an Office Clown

You may think your office has enough clowns already. You may be right. While I don't know your office, you do. But here, I'm talking about an "official" clown. Someone who actually dresses like a clown (on purpose) and acts like a clown (on purpose). You would need to have a large organization to afford a full time clown, but then many organizations have many full time clowns on the staff who don't do half the work I'm proposing for my "official office clown."

Here is the theory: Return with me now to the Dark Ages, literally. Way, way back, the kings of Europe came up with the idea of a "court jester." The court jester had to entertain the king and his men and his important visitors. But in many places, the court jester was also allowed to make fun of the king. The court jester could say and do things in a humorous manner that would have earned the various knights and princes a beheading if they had spoken so critically of the king.

The court jester was not a fool. The court jester had to entertain, but also had to point out to the king, in a friendly, humorous, non-threatening way, when the king was foolish and needed to change his policies.

The king's advisors would frequently come to the court jester in secret and ask his assistance in pointing out some of the king's follies. The jester could make points that the advisors dared not discuss. Of course, more than one court jester got a quick trip to the guillotine too, but many times their humorous remarks resulted in the king changing a bad policy so as not to appear foolish to all his subjects.

My theory of Western Civilization maintains that the reason England became the dominant power in the world and created the greatest empire that ever existed was not just because of its navy, but because it had the funniest, smartest court jesters in all of Europe.

Okay, understand the idea? Your office has an "official clown" or court jester who roams about the office complex doing funny things for managers and employees, but also observing what is going on, listening to what employees are talking about, and understanding their concerns. The clown also attends top staff meetings and is permitted (encouraged) to be silly and attack new proposals and projects in a humorous, silly manner that would never be tolerated from regular division managers. The clown is encouraged to say to the CEO what the managers would like to say, but dare not.

Try it. If you don't agree that this idea results in a thousand laughs and at least a 20 percent increase in overall efficiency, send the clown to the guillotine.

Fun Idea Number 88

Have an Office Cheerleader

If you can have an office clown, why not an office cheerleader? Many managers and staff assistants are little more than cheerleaders. They go around saying the equivalent of "rah-rah" every time the boss opens his or her mouth. This sort of thing makes me sick. But since it seems inevitable, why not designate one person to be the official cheerleader and everyone else can stop this annoying nonsense. Seriously, a certain amount of cheerleading can be beneficial to an organization, but most do it poorly. So let's have a professional; let's get a specialist.

This person (man or woman) could actually wear a cheerleader's outfit. They could go around the complex doing chants, leading songs, making inspirational speeches, and pointing out the charts showing a rise in productivity. They can do all of this in an intentionally exaggerated manner that makes the points in a humorous and entertaining way.

Like most cheerleaders, this person should be young, attractive, energetic and not too smart. This way, if the cheerleader concept doesn't work out for your organization, you can always make this person a receptionist or a vice-president.

Fun Idea Number 89

Meditation Classes

Meditation is not necessarily fun, although it can be. But meditation does lay the groundwork for having lots of fun and for handling day-to-day hassles in the office in so that the hassles don't become major problems and result in a negative work environment. I believe that everyone should meditate. Meditation has nothing to do with any specific religion. There are many different meditation techniques. You can find a technique that's compatible with your religion and with your personality. Meditation can help you on the job and in your private life.

Because meditation is something that can help you and your employees in so many ways, you should consider having on-site, on-the-clock meditation classes. Okay, here it comes. Ready for the next commercial? I teach a class on meditation called "Meditation for Managers." This class is for managers and employees alike who wish to learn simple meditation techniques to use on the job, improve their work performance, and help them deal with the hassles and frustrations of daily office life.

While my class is helpful (and I hope you'll consider it) there are hundreds of excellent meditation instructors around the country who can also present similar classes for your organization. These classes are usually offered through various adult education and alternative education sources. They are generally inexpensive and very short. My own class is two to three hours. Learning meditation techniques is easy. Doing them takes a bit of practice. But you don't need months and months of training. A few hours of practice will suffice.

If a class is not a viable option for some reason, then buy a copy of David Harp's excellent book, *The Three-Minute Meditator*, for each of your employees. This is a short, easy-to-read, easy-to-understand book which teaches you 30 "three-minute" meditations, most of which are ideal for the working environment.

There are meditations to do while you drive to work, meditations to do while you eat lunch, and meditations to do throughout the day when you're in the restroom, a meeting, or walking the hallways. It offers the best introduction to meditation I've ever seen. Buy it. Use it. You'll feel happier at work and at home.

A few offices have even set up meditation rooms for their employees. This is a commendable idea and if you have the space and money, please consider it. However, I think the "three minute meditation techniques" are more important than a meditation room. The key is to be able to meditate almost anytime and anywhere to help yourself handle the routine daily hassles. Retreating to a meditation room (or a monastery) for longer periods of meditation may be useful on an occasional basis, but the most important thing is to use quick, effective meditations when and where you need them in your daily life.

Fun Idea Number 90

Fun Books for Employees

Obviously, I love books. I enjoy writing and reading them. In addition to those I've already recommended, here are some other fun books about work I want to recommend for you and your employees. There are many funny books on working and managing. The ones I'm recommending combine both features. They're fun to read and also provide insights into the working world. They all make great employee prizes and awards. Here's a list:

- *What's So Funny About Business?* by Sidney Harris. This is a collection of business related cartoons. They are very funny and many make excellent points as well. I've used several of his witty cartoons in this book.

- *Management In Small Doses* by Russell Ackoff. This is a series of brief essays on business and management. Each one is entertaining and informative. An excellent book. Each of your managers should have a copy of this book.

- *A Whack On The Side of The Head* by Roger von Oech. This is a book on creativity in the work environment. It focuses on ten "mental locks" that frequently block creativity and provides ways to unlock your mind for innovation. An excellent combination of wit, humor and practical ideas.

Fun Idea Number 91

Apply "New Age" Management Techniques

As I noted in the Introduction, you can't "paper over" a repressive work environment with a few fun activities. The ideas in this listing will only work where the basic structure for a fun work environment has already been put in place. If you treat your employees like dirt and pay them with dirt, you can't expect that they will sing and dance and be happy just because you hold some silly contest or give them a silly prize.

In *Working and Managing In the New Age,* I spelled out in some detail the fundamentals of "New Age Management" and the process whereby an organization treats employees like whole, adult, human beings. This is the starting point for a fun work environment. If you deny a mother time off to take her child to his first day of school (as a manager in our office did one day), you shouldn't be surprised that this woman is repulsed at receiving computer generated jokes while working at her terminal.

We must begin by treating employees decently and honorably. Once we've established the basic framework, then some of these fun and games ideas will make the office a happier, more productive place. But without that basic foundation, these fun games will be insulting, degrading and totally counter-productive. Let me briefly summarize the fundamental concepts of New Age Management.

1. Holistic

The foremost aspect of New Age Management is a "holistic" approach to employees. Simply put, this concept involves treating employees as whole people, not just an another unit of production.

2. Fun

Fun is one of the most important features of New Age Management. Therefore, it has been the theme of this entire book.

3. Meaningful

People need to feel that what they are doing matters. Management must constantly remind employees of the importance of their jobs, remind them of the "big picture" and how their work fits into that overall picture. For a job to be "meaningful," it need not necessarily involve major issues of great historical significance. However, the job must make sense to the person doing it.

4. Positive Feedback

The importance of positive feedback can't be overstated. A manager who is effective at providing sincere, positive feedback will need to do little else to be successful.

5. Participatory Management

The New Age organization has an open decision-making process. There is a high degree of employee involvement.

6. Flexibility

The New Age Manager puts people ahead of procedures. If the rigid application of company policy would result in an injustice, then the manager finds a way around the policy. The effective manager knows when and how to make exceptions to general practices.

7. Open, Honest Communications

An organization that has open lines of communication with valid, honest information going up, down and throughout the organization will be much more effective and a much better place to work than the organization that attempts to restrict the flow of information or distort it and deceive people.

8. Three Dimensional Perspective

The New Age Manager is able to see beyond the immediate and beyond the obvious. The New Age Manager considers the broad impact of a decision. Understanding the universe to be a unified process or system, the New Age Manager knows that changing one thing sets off a "ripple effect" which generates many other changes in many other places.

9. Minimal Use of Coercion

Most employees will not perform at their optimum level under the constant threat of punishment. The New Age Manager generally uses power as a last resort. He or she knows that rewards are a better motivator than punishments (the carrot always beats the stick).

10. Minimal Layers of Management

Many organizations have too many levels of managers and reducing these layers is one of the essential steps in improving productivity and employee morale. This is not just a question of eliminating unnecessary positions. It also involves de-centralizing authority to local levels so that meaningful employee participation can occur. The objective is to have self-management to the extent possible and not over-management.

11. Equalitarian

The New Age organization seeks to minimize barriers between managers and employees and reduce unnecessary status symbols.

12. Developmental

The New Age organization is dedicated to helping its employees grow as workers and as people.

13. Positive Orientation to Change

An organization with a positive view of change creates a natural system rather than a mechanical system. The more easily an organization can adapt to change (internal and external) the more natural it is and the greater its chances of long-term success and survival.

Fun Idea Number 92

Coffee Pots in the Work Units

I hope you already do this. I'm mentioning it because it's one of my pet peeves. In many offices, including the one where I work, if you want a cup of coffee, tea or decaf, you have to either get on an elevator and spend ten minutes going to the cafeteria or go to the vending machine on the floor. If you have the correct change, you can buy a third-rate cup of coffee, assuming the machine is working that day. This is no way to run an office.

I used to work at an office in New York City where each unit (about 15 to 20 people) was allowed to have its own coffee pots. We had three (one regular, one unleaded and one with hot water for tea). This cost the employer nothing beyond electricity. The employees bought the coffee pots and brought in the coffee, sugar, sweeteners, etc. We took turns cleaning out the pots. A small thing, yet it made working in this office so much nicer. Whenever you wanted a cup of coffee, you just walked a few feet and poured yourself one.

It's little things like this that can make a big difference. The office I presently work in refuses to allow us to do this because, among other reasons, it would hurt the business of the man who runs the on-site cafeteria. I think an organization should be more concerned about employee morale and productivity than subsidizing the cafeteria owner or nearby restaurants.

Fun Idea Number 93

Nerf™ Basketball

I'm the only person in my office with a basketball goal in my office. It isn't a real basketball goal. My ceiling isn't high enough for that. It's a Nerf basketball goal. It slips easily over the door. Whenever I'm working on a difficult case or trying to come up with ideas for my next presentation, I find it helps me relax and think of things if I shoot a few Nerf baskets. So I just pull my little foam ball out of my desk drawer and pop a few baskets.

Of course, I close the door to my office first, so everyone else doesn't think I'm just goofing off. This technique has helped me develop several successful ideas. If you like shooting baskets, you should have your own Nerf goal. If you have a friend in the office who also likes to play, you can do a little "one on one" from time to time.

Don't think of this as just shooting baskets. Think of it as shooting down the barriers to creativity. Or at least that's what you can tell your boss.

Fun Idea Number 94

Hang a Smoker

I don't smoke. I may as well admit my prejudices right up front. I never did smoke. Even as a little kid, before I had heard about all the scientific evidence, I knew instinctively that it couldn't possibly be for good for your health to suck smoke into your body. Now with the evidence proving beyond all reasonable doubt that smoking is bad for smokers and a threat to non-smokers as well, it's clear that we must restrict smoking in the work place.

I believe no organization should permit smoking. The company where I work has banned smoking in all of its offices throughout the nation. Still, the smokers continue to rip us off. Now they spend half their time outside on unofficial smoke breaks forcing non-smokers (80 percent of our employees) to do more than their fair share of the work.

Nevertheless, this is better than having them smoking in the office and threatening the health and safety of innocent human beings.

Anyway, here's a fun idea: If you have someone in your office who smokes and pollutes your air or if you have someone who takes an unfair number of breaks to go outside and continue their nasty, disgusting habit, then hang them. If they want to die, let's help them. Let's get it over with. None of this slow suicide stuff. One quick jerk and be done with it.

Of course, the major drawback to this idea is that you may be sent to prison. Our society does not yet recognize that hanging smokers is actually a laudable environmental protection measure which should be encouraged and rewarded. So, don't totally kill them. Just tie them up, put them up on a chair, kick it out, let them hang for just a few seconds until they start to turn purple, then cut them down. After they've experienced a few seconds without oxygen, they'll understand why the rest of us value clean oxygen so much. Who knows? This may even motivate them to stop smoking. In years to come, they'll probably thank you.

P.S. This was not a serious suggestion. But wouldn't it be fun? A possible alternative is to hang the smoker in effigy. Or better yet, burn them in effigy. Or put on a company-paid stop-smoking course and show them you love them.

P.P.S. If you work for a tobacco company, don't even bring this idea up.

Fun Idea Number 95

Create Your Own Cartoons

Oh, that's right, you can't draw. Me either. But that's not an insurmountable problem. Let me explain how to develop your own cartoons even if you can't draw. Have you ever heard of "clip art?" This is your key.

Clip art consists of art work which is copyright-free. It is used by advertisers all the time. You can buy sheets of various drawings or entire books with hundreds of different drawings for you to use on almost any topic. You can get books filled with men's faces, women's face, couples in romantic situations, travel situations, business situations, office situations, restaurant and food drawings, cowboys, military, etc. You can purchase a book (usually for only a few dollars) with hundreds of drawings on any topic.

You can get these drawings through local art supply stores, typesetters or order them through various mail-order suppliers. One of the largest supplies of clip art is Dover Publications, 31 East 2nd Street, Mineola, New York 11501. They have dozens of books on almost every conceivable subject.

Once you have your clip art, you simply find an appropriate drawing and add your own language (tag line). The words can be added immediately below the drawing or if the words are supposed to be something spoken by the person or character in the drawing you can add a cartoon balloon and put the words inside.

By the way, you can buy blank sheets of these as well.

So the only difficult thing you have to do is write something clever to go with your drawing. But this is the fun and creative part that gives you an opportunity to say something specifically relevant and tailored to your work situation. It's unlikely you'll ever find a cartoon in *The Far Side* or *Doonesbury* which actually has the names of employees in your organization, but you can create your own cartoons using specific names, work units and situations from your office environment. Just be sure the cartoons are not something that will offend people.

Let me give you some examples of how I have used this. At one point we had a decision-making process which we called "the DMP" which was, in my opinion, a bad joke. We would spend hundreds of hours discussing trivial decisions but never discuss major decisions at all. I took a big picture of a silly clown and simply had the clown say "I love the DMP." Everyone knew what it meant. It became a symbol used by all of us who opposed the DMP. Even the supporters of the DMP liked the cartoon and thought it was better than hearing another speech about how stupid the DMP was.

Below is an another example of a cartoon I created. It's obviously not as good as a professional cartoon, but it was directly relevant to my audience and for that purpose was better than anything I could have used from elsewhere. To protect the innocent and guilty (and shield me from law suits) I have changed the names for this book, but I used real names at the time. I used this cartoon in a presentation at a conference on morale.

This particular organization was managed at the time by a "triumvirate" — which is to say they had three officers who shared power. Two of them were far removed from my ideal of a "New Age" manager. The third was an intelligent, perceptive individual but new to the officer's position and only there on a temporary basis. He was subject to being removed at any time and had to be very careful.

Everyone with eyes to see, ears to hear, and a brain to think knew this particular organization had a major morale problem but the two top managers were unwilling to take any significant steps to address what was truly a crisis situation. It was at this point in time that I created this cartoon.

Now this cartoon obviously doesn't do much for you, but it was a big hit among the managers and employees of this organization. The point is that it's relatively easy for you to use clip art and create meaningful cartoons for your organizations. You can then use the cartoons on your memos, handouts, etc. Try it. It's fun.

Fun Idea Number 96

A Stick Pin Doll

Are you familiar with voodoo? Do you believe that sticking pins into a little doll representing your enemy will actually cause your enemy pain? Well, I should hope not. But you can have some fun with this idea anyway. Have your art department make you a little cushion doll that looks like one of your major enemies. Perhaps it's your competitor, a union president, or the leader of your home office.

Place the doll and lots of pins in a convenient, private location where most managers can have access to the doll. Each time the "doll" does something stupid to cost you money, time and energy, take a pin and shove it in. You will have so much fun doing this that you may even temporarily forget about the latest atrocity this person has committed.

Now, as I confessed early in the book, I'm somewhat skeptical about unions. I feel that the modern organization needs unions about as much as a fish needs a bicycle. I have seen too many goof-offs hiding behind the union label for me to ever be naive about unions.

In my very first job right out of graduate school, I was a union member and worked with the union to organize a national strike. The union sold out the employees to protect its own institutional interests and I've been cynical ever since, especially when I hear some union leader talking about his deep concern for the working people when his only real concern is making sure that he never has to become a working person himself.

In addition, on a number of occasions, I've seen management want to give employees a new benefit and the union insist the benefit be delayed for several months (or years) until the contract comes up for renegotiation, all so the union could get credit for "winning" the new benefit at the bargaining table. Once again, the union leaders were primarily concerned about the union itself, not the workers.

Now I recognize there are many notable exceptions and there are many fine unionists. I have worked for the past two decades with many outstanding union people and respect several of them. But even the best unionists can get on your nerves sometimes, especially during their elections when they go into some of their phony political routines. A little union stick doll can be a lot of fun for people who feel the way I do.

If you don't have a union, of if you have a responsible union that works with you rather than against you, then use the stick pin doll idea for someone else. Perhaps your chief competitor or your CEO?

Fun Idea Number 97

Self-Image Therapy

Your self-image is critical. Do you see yourself as a pawn on the board of life, someone who is moved here and there with no rhyme or reason and who has no control over your own destiny? If so, then you will be a passive patsy and the organization will eat up your spirit and spit you out for the dogs. On the other hand, if you see yourself as an active agent for change, as someone in control of your own happiness and state of mind, then you can become a social revolutionary and help create a better world for yourself and your co-workers.

And when you do begin to see yourself as an agent for change, as a social revolutionary, as a positive force for a better organization and a better world, as an "Aquarian Conspirator" or "Peaceful Warrior" or whatever label you prefer, when you willfully begin to create your own reality by seeking to create a better work environment, then you will see that "fun" and "humor" (along with love and compassion and understanding) are two of your major weapons in your quest. A better world will be a world with more fun. Fun is not frivolous. Fun is an essential ingredient of any true revolution including the revolution in the work place.

One of the most practical steps you can take towards creating a more positive work situation and towards creating fun in the workplace, is to begin to think of yourself as an active force for a better work environment. Don't wait for someone else to start the revolution. Don't wait for someone else to start the fun. Fun is revolutionary. Have some today!

"Happy days are here again.
The shares you hold have split again.
We plan to raise the dividend.
Happy days are here again!"

Fun Idea Number 98

Video Games

Perhaps you would rather be tarred and feathered than have to play a video game. But many people love video games, including yours truly. I find them relaxing. I "meditate" while playing Pac-Man™, Space Invaders™, etc. After a few rounds, I feel refreshed and more creative. I know many other people react the same way. Therefore, it would seem a worthy idea to have a video game room in your office where employees can go over lunch, at break or perhaps even occasionally during work time to play a few games and relax.

I recommend a separate room because some games are very noisy, but an alternative idea is to install video games in your computer system so that people can call up the games at their desks and play on their own terminals. These games would have to be quiet (unless everyone has a separate office), but it could be a refreshing change of pace after keying data for two hours to call up a computer black jack game or a you-vs-the computer basketball game. If you don't want employees tempted all day long, put a timer on so the games could only be called up during lunch or other non-work periods. If you already have the hardware, the software for the games is inexpensive and will help people have a more positive attitude towards their PCs.

Fun Idea Number 99

An Office Treasure Hunt

Do you remember treasure hunts? I remember them as a kid, but that was years ago. Anyway, for those of you who have never been on a treasure hunt, let me briefly explain.

You begin with a treasure. It can be anything. It can be something valuable (like a hundred dollar bill) or something silly (like Betty Lou's coffee cup). Someone hides the object. This person also writes many clues directing you towards other clues directing you towards the object. Each clue leads you towards another clue until finally you find the hidden treasure. All the contestants start together at one point and race to see who can figure out the clues to find the next clues to find the next clues to finally find the object. The winner is the first person or first group (if you play groups, which is more fun) to find the object.

Now, this game can be applied to the office with fun and some value as well. How many of your managers have ever been to the mail room? Not many, I would guess. Hide the object somewhere and have the clues send the players throughout the entire organization so that they have to go to the mailroom for one clue, the printing room for another clue, the maintenance room for another clue, etc. It's a fun game and it gets people out and about to explore all the nooks and crannies of the office complex.

There are numerous variations on this theme. If you manage a legal research team, give them a particular case to find and see who finds it first. If you supervise a team of quality inspectors, put a bad part in an area where you know where it is and see which inspector can find it first. Almost anything can be turned into a game. And games are more fun than work even when you perform the identical activities in each. It's all in the context. Create a fun context.

"Let's face it—we have no quality and we have no control."

Fun Idea Number 100

An Office Decathlon

The decathlon is an Olympic contest that features 10 separate track and field events. If you can come in second or third in all ten activities, you may well win the decathlon even though you weren't the best in any one event. The decathlon winner is considered a good all-around athlete. You can apply this concept to your organization. Have a competition combining three, five or even ten different work related activities. These competitions can be individual, but it may be more fun to have teams.

For example, establish several different teams. Give them an assignment (a real work assignment or a phony one) which requires research, math calculations, writing a memo, typing a memo, reviewing the memo, photocopying the memo, distributing the memo, etc. The first person or team to complete the entire range of activities and turn in an acceptable work product wins the office decathlon. Depending upon what functions your organization performs, you can change the specific activities.

Even if you don't have teams, it's still interesting to see how versatile people are in certain situations. For example, does the chief executive get stuck trying to type his own memo and lose to his secretary who knows how to do research, write, type, photo and deliver. If so, how much quality was lost in the memo? You may discover you can eliminate the executive and have the secretary do it all. Or if you play this game as a team, why are some groups able to work together better than others? Is it strictly talent? Or is it the division of responsibility within the team or communications within the team?

Again, this is a game. It is fun. But it can provide some interesting insights into your own organization.

"I'm seriously thinking of getting three new younger, brighter idiots."

Fun Idea Number 101

A Pie Fighting Contest

Few things in life are more fun than a pie fight. Yet, when was the last time you had a pie fight? Many years, I dare to guess. Picture this, your sales department vs. your accounting department with 100 whipped cream pies on each side. If this isn't a media event, I don't know what is. If you prefer to avoid publicity (and I can see how you might), this would still be a lot of fun.

Variations include a water gun war, pillow fights, Nerf™ sword fights, a tug of war, and a mud wrestling contest. Remember when you were a toddler? Probably not. Well, remember your own kids when they were toddlers? I'm sure you do. Remember how much fun it was to get real, real messy. Well, that's the idea here. Let's get messy. Let's have some fun. Let's go back to the "terrible twos" and have one more blast.

Fun Idea Number 102

(A Bonus Idea)

Have a Pep Rally

Hey, wait! There were only supposed to be a 101 ideas. What's happening? Let me explain. The number "101" is apparently a good marketing concept. Thus, a book titled "101 Ways to Cut Taxes" or "101 Ways to Have Better Sex" is allegedly more likely to sell than a book called "92 Ways to Cut Taxes" or "106 Ways to Have Better Sex." I don't know for a fact that this marketing idea is true. I'm not sure that "101" is a magic number, but everyone else seems to think so.

But I have more than 101 ideas. I have thousands of ideas. Now I'm not going to tell you all my ideas. I need to save a few surprises for my workshops and a few ideas for my sequel Making Work Even More Fun: Another 101 Ways to Increase Morale, Cut Taxes, and Have Better Sex. (Just kidding, there is no such sequel — at least not yet.)

However, I do want to share a few more ideas with you and I'm not going to stop just because we are at the magic number of 101. Besides, you probably hated a few of the 101 ideas and feel you should get a few free replacement ideas to compensate you.

So here goes: Your first bonus idea is a pep rally. This is another idea taken from my high school and college days. You can develop a lot of interesting ideas for the work environment by taking ideas from other areas and applying them to work and seeing if they make any sense. The pep rally may or may not make sense for your organization, but some companies have done this effectively.

You can do this some Friday night after work or some night just before a big meeting or sales conference the next day. Have a bonfire. Have cheerleaders. Burn the competition in effigy. Sing songs. Steal the competitions' mascot (or better yet, their Swiss bank account). Invite the press and get some free publicity for your organization. Picture the Big Eight Accounting Firms having pep rallies the night before the tax forms are sent out. Picture General Motors having a pep rally the night before a new plant opens. You get the idea; now use it. Or burn it in the bonfire if you think that's a more appropriate use of the idea.

Another Bonus Idea

Dunk the CEO

This is an old gimmick from carnivals and county fairs. You take someone (such as a CEO or division manager) towards whom many employees have essentially repressed feelings of anxiety and let them release their aggressions and feelings by throwing a ball at a target which, if hit, will release the seat where the CEO is sitting and thereby dunk him or her in a pool of water.

Any manager who goes along with this idea is a good sport and will likely score lots of points with the employees each time he or she gets dunked. Employees usually have to pay a dollar to get three balls to throw at the target and the money can go to charity. Everyone has fun and the company gets to raise some money for charity and probably get some publicity as well.

To be honest, if I were the CEO, I'd send one of my most disliked vice-presidents for this assignment.

A Bonus Potpourri

What?

Here are some simple ideas that require little explanation:

A. Decorate Your Office With Balloons

Balloons create a festive, fun, party-like atmosphere. Buy a hundred, blow them up and hang them around. They'll do wonders for morale and lung capacity.

B. Decorate Your Office With Plants and Flowers

C. Have an Open House

Open the office some Saturday and let everyone bring in their friends, family and kids and show off where they work.

D. Have A T-Shirt Contest

The most original or humorous shirt wins a prize. Or use T-shirts with company slogans as prizes for some of your games.

E. Establish an Exercise Club

If you don't have appropriate facilities, consider a Walking Club where employees go for walks together over lunch.

Another Bonus Idea

Yo-Yos

Your office probably has dozens of yo-yos, but they aren't the kind I'm talking about. I'm referring to the little round objects that go up and down on a string. How many years has it been since you played with a yo-yo? Were you ever able to get one to "sleep?" Could you get it to go "Around the World?" It's never too late to learn or re-learn these fun yo-yo techniques. There are now various versions of "any idiot can yo-yo" books. My favorite is *The Klutz Yo-Yo Book* by John Cassidy.

Here's the idea: Have someone on your staff read *The Klutz Yo-Yo Book* and learn to yo-yo. Then someday over lunch, get everyone who's interested together and teach them a few simple yo-yo tricks. Then the next time you have a semi-important meeting with someone from outside your local organization, have everyone bring their yo-yos. Just before this outside person is ready to speak, the entire staff stands up, pulls out their yo-yos and does their favorite trick. This is guaranteed to put your outside visitor at ease (or something).

However, don't try this if your outside visitor is a potential buyer for your product (unless you make yo-yos). He or she may think you're all a bunch of yo-yos and walk out. I would save this idea for someone who is trying to sell something (a product or an idea) to your organization.

Not only will this little yo-yo demonstration help put your

visitor at ease, it will also clearly establish that your organization is a fun place to work and that his or her product or idea had better fit in with your theme.

Question: Is this a serious suggestion?

Answer: Semi-serious. Some of these ideas are more fun to think about than actually do. However, it is possible that the yo-yo idea might be appropriate for a particular type of meeting. In any event, I wanted to list a few totally bizarre ideas just to get you thinking. There are thousands of possibilities for injecting fun into the work environment.

Use your imagination and you might be able to think of a meeting where the yo-yo idea would be effective. Or you can think of an alternative to the yo-yo idea which would be just as much fun but more appropriate to your organization and your specific type of meeting.

Another Bonus Idea

Harmonica Blues

This is an idea for establishing a "learning curve" for your employees. That is, while having some fun, you can learn which of your employees are quick studies. Eliminate anyone from the study who already knows how to play the harmonica or who is a musical expert. Then, give each employee a copy of David Harp's excellent package, *Instant Blues Harmonica* which contains a harmonica, a tape, and a book. This is a self-study guide for the harmonica. Allow each employee two weeks or 30 days to study and practice on their own time (I learned to play in my car commuting to and from work) and then have an office "blues jam."

Your employees will have fun learning. They will have fun for years to come playing their harmonicas for their friends and family. And you'll quickly see which of your employees can learn an entirely alien subject matter quickly. This could prove very important to you at some point when your office has to install a new computer or telephone system and you don't have anyone with expertise in that area. You must be able to select someone who can quickly learn a brand new subject.

Still Another Bonus Idea

The Office Turkey

We've discussed numerous ideas for recognizing and rewarding good performance through various awards. This idea is exactly the opposite. Here, you give an award (The Golden Turkey) to someone to highlight poor performance in the hopes of making sure it never happens again. This is along the lines of the Golden Fleece Award that former Senator William Proxmire used to present from time to time to a government agency wasting taxpayer money on some particularly stupid program.

This award will not be fun to the person who gets it, but it will be fun to everyone else. Make no mistake about it, this can be a malicious award. You should give this considerable thought before doing it. It may be counterproductive. It should not be issued on a regular basis, only when something outrageous occurs which requires an outlandish response.

The award could be given to an individual or a group. If your office or plant in Cleveland has been the least productive unit in the nation for 28 years in a row, give them the Golden Turkey. If the new vice-president smashes into the side of the CEO's antique Rolls Royce, it's Golden Turkey time. The award can be given good-naturedly or maliciously. It's usually handed to someone who has done something outrageous but not an offense justifying termination. If termination is in order, fire them. Don't bother with the Golden Turkey.

But if you want to keep the person and give them a kick in the head they will never forget for an action you intend that they never, ever repeat, consider the Golden Turkey.

Then, again, you may have someone you would like to fire but can't. Maybe they have an iron-clad employment contract which prohibits terminations. Maybe you have a union agreement which makes it impossible to fire the person. Maybe you just don't want to risk litigation. Maybe you work for a public agency (a school system or the federal government) where it's next to impossible to fire anyone. In these situations, presenting the Golden Turkey may motivate this incompetent employee to resign or retire.

Plus, every organization seems to have a few pompous jerks, who while not totally incompetent, need a kick in the seat of the pants from time to time. Let your Golden Turkey do the kicking.

One variation some organizations use is to have a "secret committee" nominate and select the Golden Turkey and present the award anonymously and without fanfare. So the "turkey" simply arrives at the office one day to find the award in a sealed envelop. There is no presentation. There is no announcement. There is no publicity. There is no picture for the company newsletter. But the turkey has the award and understands why. You may feel this whole idea is demeaning and dehumanizing. You may be right. But I'm sure you can think of at least a dozen people in your organization who deserve such an award. Just the fantasy of presenting them such an award should bring you a little fun – or a little guilty pleasure.

There are dozens of possibilities for the Golden Turkey Award, but you must be careful. When you play with this turkey, you're playing with fire.

P.S. If you work for a company that sells real turkeys to the supermarkets, you may want to rename this the "Bozo Award."

A Final Bonus Idea

The Yearbook

By now, you may think that I'm the office turkey. You may think these bonus ideas are turkeys. You may feel the quality of these last few ideas has been so poor that I should have stopped at 101. You may be right. Well, I have good news for you. This is your final idea in this listing.

This is an idea for any organization. Do you know what the people who work in your organization look like? Do you know their personal interests? If you work in a small organization, the answer is probably "yes." But if your office has thousands of employees, you probably don't know who many of them are. Our office has had up to 2,000 employees at various times. I never knew more than a few hundred at most. Yet, because I have a highly visible job, many of them knew me and spoke to me by name. I always wanted a way to put names with faces and learn just a little bit about the people that I spoke to.

Okay, there's the idea. Remember high school? You know that place you went every day for four years to learn and practice the latest seduction techniques? Remember the yearbook? Remember all those pictures that are so much fun to go back and look at now? Your organization can create its own yearbook.

Once a year, take a picture of each employee (voluntary participation only, but I can't imagine that more than a few spoil-sports will decline to participate), have them tell you a few basic facts about themselves (their job position, their outside interests, how many children they have, etc.) and put this into a yearbook. Provide free copies to each employee.

Most large organizations already publish a telephone directory, so employees can contact one another. Why not make the directory into a yearbook and get an extra benefit?

You'll be surprised how valuable this book is. If you want to know who someone is, where they work, or what their interests are, just look them up in the yearbook. If you're looking for a co-worker who shares your interest in chess, check out the yearbook. If you're looking for an attractive person for a passionate relationship, scan your yearbook.

If you want to know the names of the people who say "hello" to you in the elevator, check them out in the yearbook. Save the yearbooks in your office library. Ten or twenty years down the road, it will be a real treat to go back and see how everyone has degenerated with age. It's a thousand laughs. I guarantee it.

CHAPTER 4

One Last Laugh

I hope you've enjoyed reading this book. I was sometimes flippant. I was sometimes nasty. I was sometimes cynical and sarcastic. I meant every word.

No, not really. I wanted the book to be fun for you so I periodically went a step or two beyond good taste and logical thinking. Some of the things I said I didn't mean. Some of them (like hang a smoker) were obvious, others perhaps less so.

But the book had two objectives. First, I wanted you to enjoy reading it so you would continue. Second, I wanted you to think about fun and work and how the two can be integrated. If you have reached this concluding section, then my first objective has been achieved; you did keep reading.

Now, while I hope you had lots of laughs reading the book, I hope you will go on to the next step. I don't know where the bookstores will stock this book. They may put it in the humor section or the business section (or hopefully both). But let me assure you that this book is serious.

I believe work should be fun. I believe many (although certainly not all) of the ideas in this book will be helpful to you in creating a positive work environment. I sincerely urge you to try some of these ideas. I urge you especially to consider ideas number 20, 21, 22. (Do a Morale Survey, Create a Morale Committee, Appoint a Morale Manager.)

Don't just file this book away in your library. It wasn't just meant to be merely an entertainment. This book was meant to give you specific ideas for revolutionizing your work environment. Take these ideas and start your own revolution.

I'm convinced that if you try some of these ideas you'll make your work environment more efficient and less stressful. Conduct a scientific experiment. Try one of the ideas and see what happens. And while you're at it — Have Fun!